Cambridge Elements

Elements on Women in the History of Philosophy
edited by
Jacqueline Broad
Monash University

IRIS MURDOCH

Bridget Clarke
University of Montana

Shaftesbury Road, Cambridge CB2 8EA, United Kingdom

One Liberty Plaza, 20th Floor, New York, NY 10006, USA

477 Williamstown Road, Port Melbourne, VIC 3207, Australia

314–321, 3rd Floor, Plot 3, Splendor Forum, Jasola District Centre, New Delhi – 110025, India

103 Penang Road, #05–06/07, Visioncrest Commercial, Singapore 238467

Cambridge University Press is part of Cambridge University Press & Assessment, a department of the University of Cambridge.

We share the University's mission to contribute to society through the pursuit of education, learning and research at the highest international levels of excellence.

www.cambridge.org
Information on this title: www.cambridge.org/9781009571739

DOI: 10.1017/9781009358156

© Bridget Clarke 2025

This publication is in copyright. Subject to statutory exception and to the provisions of relevant collective licensing agreements, no reproduction of any part may take place without the written permission of Cambridge University Press & Assessment.

When citing this work, please include a reference to the DOI 10.1017/9781009358156

First published 2025

A catalogue record for this publication is available from the British Library

ISBN 978-1-009-57173-9 Hardback
ISBN 978-1-009-35814-9 Paperback
ISSN 2634-4645 (online)
ISSN 2634-4637 (print)

Cambridge University Press & Assessment has no responsibility for the persistence or accuracy of URLs for external or third-party internet websites referred to in this publication and does not guarantee that any content on such websites is, or will remain, accurate or appropriate.

Iris Murdoch

Elements on Women in the History of Philosophy

DOI: 10.1017/9781009358156
First published online: March 2025

Bridget Clarke
University of Montana
Author for correspondence: Bridget Clarke, bclarke@mso.umt.edu

Abstract: Iris Murdoch is well-known for her moral philosophy, especially for the light it sheds on the inner life. This Element focuses on the political significance and contours of Murdoch's ethics. Its chief aim is to illuminate the affinities between Murdoch's concept of the individual and the Enlightenment ideal of a society in which people live together as free equals. There are five sections in this Element. Section 1 provides context for the discussion. Section 2 compares what Murdoch calls the liberal and naturalistic outlooks and argues that she develops a modified version of the naturalistic outlook to better support an Enlightenment sensibility. Sections 3 and 4 examine the three main features of Murdoch's "naturalized" individual. Section 3 considers the individual's uniqueness and transcendence. Section 4 considers the individual's knowability through love. Section 5 offers some concluding remarks.

Keywords: Iris Murdoch, individual, liberalism, love, political

© Bridget Clarke 2025

ISBNs: 9781009571739 (HB), 9781009358149 (PB), 9781009358156 (OC)
ISSNs: 2634-4645 (online), 2634-4637 (print)

Contents

1 The Political Significance of Murdoch's Moral Thought   1

2 The Individual and Her Background   10

3 The Unique and Transcendent Individual   30

4 The Individual Revealed by Love   41

5 Concluding Remarks   56

   Abbreviations of Works by Murdoch   58

   References   60

1 The Political Significance of Murdoch's Moral Thought

In philosophy we go where the honey is. Some thinkers are, for us, living and life-giving.[1]

1.1 Introduction

Iris Murdoch (1919–1999) was both a celebrated novelist and an exceptionally original philosopher. At a time when moral philosophy in both Europe and the Anglophone world was in thrall to subjectivism, Murdoch went another way entirely, drawing on Plato, Kant, Hegel, Freud, Sartre, Simone Weil, and Wittgenstein to recast the idea of virtue, or goodness, as knowledge. Murdoch identified goodness with the ability to see things, situations, and, above all, people in ways undistorted by how one fears them to be, or expects them to be, or would like them to be. And she linked this capacity for clear-sightedness to a loving awareness of human variety, vulnerability, and limitation. Readers of many different kinds have found in Murdoch's development of these ideas an especially living and life-giving picture of moral life.

Such a picture certainly seems well-suited to contribute to our thinking about politics, about how we can best live with others in the social world, or worlds, we share. Murdoch herself was *close* to politics in many ways, beginning with her Anglo-Irish heritage. Her parents moved from Dublin to London shortly after her birth, to escape the Northern Ireland conflict, and never fully integrated into English society. Murdoch was, and remained, keenly aware of being Irish in England. As an adult Murdoch lived through World War II, the collapse of the Soviet Union, and the emergence of the postwar liberal world. She worked with war refugees through the United Nations Relief and Rehabilitation Agency (UNRRA), first in London and later in Austria and Belgium. She supported the Republican cause in Spain. She wrote with passion and acuity about the nuclear bomb, the Vietnam war, public education, socialism, and the legal status of homosexuality. She was a lifelong advocate for women's equality and gave special attention to their access to education.[2] She discussed liberalism and engaged with Marxist ideas and philosophers throughout her half-century long

---

[1] Iris Murdoch, "Manuscript on Heidegger," Iris Murdoch Archive, quoted in Browning 2018a: 44.
[2] Murdoch herself entered Oxford University in 1938, where women had only been allowed to matriculate since 1920. Once there, she had the great good fortune of undertaking her studies alongside Elizabeth Anscombe, Philippa Foot, and Mary Midgley, and doing so at a time when most men had been called to serve in World War II, thus leaving more room – psychologically as well as materially – for women to receive an education. See MacCumhaill and Wiseman 2022; Lipscombe 2021. For Murdoch's personal biography, see Conradi 2001. For a succinct overview of her philosophical career, see Broackes 2012: 1–8. Browning 2024: ch. 7 and Bolton 2022 discuss Murdoch and feminism.

career. She was at once perceptive and prescient when, at the age of twenty-eight, she described herself as having a mind "on the borders of philosophy, literature, and politics."[3]

Nevertheless, it has proven very difficult to bring the political significance and contours of Murdoch's ethics into focus. There are many reasons for this, beginning with the sheer complexity of her writings. There is also the fact that her view of the relationship between politics and ethics (along with her political views themselves) shifted over time. Above all, there is the fact that Murdoch's moral philosophy focuses, as novels often do, on the inner life.[4]

1.2 Approach

One way to develop the case for the political significance of Murdoch's ethics is to show that there is a happy convergence between what Murdoch sees as going into good moral agency or character, on the one hand, and what turns out to be needed for political progress, on the other.[5] This approach to Murdoch is accurate and illuminating on one condition: that we think of political progress as progress toward a society of free and equal people, that is, a society in which one's religion, gender, sexual orientation, ancestry, race, or worldview has no bearing whatsoever on one's political standing. In other words, what we might call "the convergence approach" to the political significance of Murdoch's ethics succeeds only if our idea of political progress is based on Enlightenment values.

This qualification marks a limitation, of course, but also potentially a strength. Precisely because Murdoch's ethics is keyed to Enlightenment political values, it helps us *see* these values and helps us to consider, in particular, the kind of mindset and practices that might serve them. This is where Murdoch's focus on the inner life arguably pays dividends.[6] How do individuals avoid attaching undue significance to

---

[3] Letter to Raymond Queneau, October 17, 1947 (Horner and Rowe 2016: 99).
[4] As a result, Murdoch's ethics has long held a reputation for being politically disengaged or negligent. Setiya calls her "philosophically apolitical" (Setiya 2024). Others charge Murdoch with a lack of interest in the social and political determinants of moral vision (Blum 2022a; Nussbaum 2001). In defense, commentators have highlighted aspects of Murdoch's philosophical writings that register the importance of the individual's social and political surround (Antonaccio 2012: ch. 12; Browning 2019, 2018a; Clarke 2012, 2006; Hämäläinen 2022, 2015; Holland 2012; Samuel 2021). A different line of criticism, put forward by Lovibond 2011, maintains that Murdoch equates virtue with self-abnegation and thereby plays into reactionary (gender) politics notwithstanding her explicit endorsement of Enlightenment values. Hämäläinen 2015 and Robjant 2011 defend Murdoch against this charge (and see 4.5.1). Browning 2024 makes a sustained case for Murdoch as a political thinker.
[5] E.g., Samuel 2021.
[6] Bearing in mind that a focus on the inner life is compatible with recognizing that collective action, structures, and institutions play an important (possibly paramount) role in determining one's mindset. Murdoch's inward focus precludes only that we are *wholly* determined by social structures. In her words: "[O]ne does not have to choose between activism and inwardness or feel that one is bound to swallow the other" (MGM: 362; also WG: 15; IP: 42).

differences in the way others look or think, especially when those differences have been stigmatized or glorified in the culture? How do they manage to keep self-interest or self-concern in some kind of check if they are not forced to do this? Murdoch's moral philosophy not only helps us to consider such questions, it was *intended* to help us to consider them. From this point of view, the political significance of Murdoch's ethics is both broad and deep. It is also timely. Climate disaster, information technology, historic income inequality, and a growing awareness of the way that liberal values have been deployed over the centuries to justify domination and exploitation, have all given new life to illiberal attitudes and movements within liberal democracies.[7] They have also made it more difficult for those who embrace liberal values to live up to them, or to be sure what doing so means here and now.

Commentators have noted the affinity between Murdoch's concept of attention and civic virtues of toleration and respect for difference.[8] In this Element I start further back, as it were, with Murdoch's concept of the individual. I bring out how this concept is keyed to Enlightenment values and how it brings many of Murdoch's other concepts in its train. Instead of beginning with attention, I end with attention. The main goal is to see Murdoch's ethics with fresh eyes and to appreciate more finely the coherence, the complexity, and the political ambitions and potential of her view.[9]

1.3 The Liberal Spirit

In pursuing this course, I will not be defending a position about whether Murdoch's philosophy is politically progressive or conservative. I examine Murdoch's philosophical writings in relation to the Enlightenment ideals of liberty, equality, and the sanctity of the individual that have traditionally been shared by progressives and conservatives alike in modern liberal democracies and that Murdoch herself embraced throughout her career.[10] There are, of course,

---

[7] The last decade has seen growing popular support for illiberal politics in Brazil, India, Britain, and many European democracies, as well as – most strikingly – the United States. As one U.S. state senator put it: "One of the [traditional] values is, if your neighbor's not hurting you, you leave them alone .... Well, what I see is less of that and more of, 'You're just going to do it my way'" (Streep 2023). On the ruthless instrumentalization of liberal values see, e.g., Elkins 2022.

[8] Antonaccio 2012: 227–228; Laverty 2022. Less directly: Clarke 2012; Spreeuwenberg 2021.

[9] My approach builds on Antonaccio's groundbreaking work (Antonaccio 2012: 45–46 and ch. 8; Antonaccio 2000: ch. 4). Antonaccio reads Murdoch as attempting to accommodate a liberal respect for the individual within a Platonic metaphysics.

[10] Murdoch's political affiliations moved from left to right over time, but her commitment to Enlightenment ideals is a constant in her published writings. In effect, she seems to have changed her mind not about the merit of these ideals but about how best to interpret or realize them. Browning 2024, 2018a and Blum 2022b discuss Murdoch's politics, her explicitly political writings, and political themes that can be found in her novels.

many different understandings of these ideals and their interrelations, but it is central to the modern interpretation of these ideals that they assign a high value to the individual's ability to frame the plan of his life to suit his own character (paraphrasing J.S. Mill), and that they assign this value equally to all individuals.[11] Crucially, this interpretation rules out zero-sum (or positional) conceptions of liberty or equality, that is, conceptions which treat liberty or equality as goods which some members of society must lack for others to possess. (The American Confederacy, for instance, conceived of liberty and equality in a way that required the existence of enslaved persons; only in contradistinction to enslaved persons, it was thought, could a white laborer be considered the equal of a white landowner.)[12] The ideals, then, entail a broad readiness to see *all* people as mattering and to allow them to lead their lives in the way that makes the most sense to them, consistent with others being allowed do the same. Murdoch called such readiness "the Liberal spirit" and took it to be at the heart of the way that great novelists approach their characters. In her words:

> A great novelist is essentially tolerant, that is, displays a real apprehension of persons other than the author as having a right to exist and to have a separate mode of being which is important and interesting to themselves . . . . . Here one may see the Liberal spirit at its best and richest disporting itself in literature (SBR: 257/271).

We should not conflate the liberal spirit with *liberalism* as Murdoch thought of it or as we do.[13] The liberal spirit refers to a broad sensibility that can be held by people from all over the social and political spectrum: resolute socialists as well as neoliberals, Christians as well as atheists. It is compatible with thinking that capitalism must (to borrow a phrase from Murdoch) "grind the faces of the poor" or that it is the best solution to poverty (HT: 172). It is *not* compatible with thinking that men should rule over women or Europeans over non-Europeans. It is anti-caste, protective of the individual, deeply democratic.[14] It recognizes the dignity of individuals per se, of their "having a right to exist and to have a separate mode of being which is important and interesting to themselves."

---

[11] Mill (1978 [1859]: 12).

[12] Coates 2015; McCurry 2020; more generally, Aziz 2010.

[13] Murdoch used the term "liberalism" (sometimes capitalized) to refer, variously, to a historical development rooted in the Enlightenment, a political theory, an intellectual tradition, and an encompassing worldview that she associated with postwar liberal democracies ("the liberal world"). The word is commonly used now to describe a wide array of positions on the political spectrum that involve a commitment to free markets and limited government, as well as to the rule of law, representative institutions of governance, and the like. Walzer 2023 draws a similar distinction between liberalism, on the one hand, and a liberal sensibility, on the other.

[14] Zakaria 1997 reminds us that democracies may be (and often have been) illiberal and that liberal states have not always been democratic. The liberal sensibility at issue here *is* democratic.

Such a sensibility holds a special – all-important – place in liberal democracies. As John Dewey put it:

> Merely legal guarantees of the civil liberties of free belief, free expression, free assembly are of little avail if in daily life freedom of communication, the give and take of ideas, facts, experiences, is choked by mutual suspicion, by abuse, by fear and hatred. These things destroy the essential condition of the democratic way of living even more effectually than open coercion (1988 [1939]: 228–229).

One of the standing threats to the liberal spirit is the desire to organize society into groups of insider and outsider, higher and lower, ruler and ruled – a desire that can be sparked or heightened when people feel disoriented, insecure, or aggrieved. In this Element I show how Murdoch offers a way for human beings to conceptualize or "picture" one another that speaks to this difficulty and that serves a liberal sensibility in other ways.

1.4 Context

Let me provide some context for this idea and then address some potential difficulties. It will be helpful to distinguish, very broadly, three periods in Murdoch's writings.

The *early* writings (1950–1961): These writings critically examine behaviorism, Sartre's existentialism, Anglophone moral philosophy; further topics include Kant's aesthetics and aesthetics more generally, socialism and liberalism.

The *middle* writings (1962–1975): These writings develop Murdoch's critique of behaviorism, existentialism, and Anglophone moral philosophy, and reflect the increasing significance for Murdoch of Plato and Simone Weil; they include the celebrated essays that comprise *The Sovereignty of Good*.

The *later* writings (1976–1992): These writings extend earlier themes and develop a critique of postmodern thought; they include *The Fire and the Sun* and the monumental *Metaphysics as a Guide to Morals*. They are the most Platonist of Murdoch's writings.

Political themes are present in each of these periods and most pervasive in the early writings. There Murdoch warned that liberal democratic societies lacked, or were at risk of losing, the concepts required to honor the ideals they stood for (SSR; HT; TSM; SBR; AD). We can relate this idea to three of Murdoch's wider commitments. (i) She took it that we naturally think in pictures. In our efforts to understand the world and our place in it, we inevitably use metaphors and imagery of various kinds (TL; NP; SGC).[15] (ii) The way that we picture the

---
[15] It's an interesting question how Murdoch's philosophy might accommodate the condition of aphantasia.

world is an extension of the *concepts* we use. So, for Murdoch, concepts shape our understanding of the world at a primal level. They shape what is thinkable for us, what we experience, and our sources of motivation (Panizza 2020; Diamond 2010; 1996; 1988). (iii) Philosophers, among others, can improve the way we picture the world by revising, refining, and enriching the concepts at our disposal. Murdoch supposes, then, that a liberal democracy needs certain concepts if its members are to be able to picture human beings and their relations with one another in a way that befits liberal values. And she thinks that philosophers have an important role to play in fulfilling this need.

We should not forget that Murdoch's concerns extended more broadly than this; she was concerned with values quite generally in the aftermath of World War II, and amid the rise of scientism and the apparent decline of religion. "[W]e are losing our sense of form and structure in the moral world itself," she wrote (AD: 293). One can read Murdoch's entire body of work as an examination of this situation and an attempt to furnish (or rescue) some of the concepts that would enable members of liberal societies to come to grips, morally and politically, with life under late capitalism (Browning 2018a; Forsberg 2013).

It is in this context that Murdoch assigned special importance to the available conceptions of the individual. Much of her work takes aim at a "romantic" conception of the individual that she took to have had a major influence in the liberal world: in its philosophy, its literature, and its politics, as well as in everyday life. Her critique thus raises the possibility that modern liberal democracies had generated a picture of the individual that was inadequate to – or even at odds with – the liberal sensibility upon which they depend. Murdoch's own conception of the individual can then be seen as an attempt to put liberal ideals on a more solid footing, while also speaking to the moral and spiritual needs of people in the modern West.

1.5 Difficulties

There are, however, some potential difficulties for the idea that Murdoch's concept of the individual has political purchase.

1. (a) Murdoch does not offer a definition of "individual" and this concept can merge, in her writings, with that of "human personality," "consciousness," or "self" (among others). (b) Her rich and evolving body of philosophical work naturally contains more than one concept of the individual.[16] So there is the danger of conflating different concepts in her work or different stages of her thought.

---

[16] In MGM Murdoch explicitly considers different concepts of the individual (350ff.). She may also be working implicitly with different concepts in her earlier work.

2. Murdoch emphasizes the variety and historicity of concepts; her sensitivity to this was at the heart of her philosophical methods and vision. She leads us to expect that the conceptual needs and resources of a society will change over time. So even if we assign political value to Murdoch's concept of the individual, it would be inappropriate to treat this concept as *the* concept of the individual that serves liberal democracy once and for all. We need to leave room for other concepts of the individual to arise both during different historical periods as well as at a given moment.[17]
3. Murdoch asks us to be careful about assigning political value to her moral philosophy.

Difficulties (1a) and (2) are basically caveats to bear in mind. (1b) and (3) require more in the way of explanation and strategy. Let's begin by considering (3).

In Murdoch's early writings, as Lawrence Blum notes, she "looks to morality to supply the ideals and values that should guide the crafting or reform of the political realm" (2022b: 427).[18] Beginning in her middle period, Murdoch becomes more wary about morality playing this role. She comes to think that a very good moral philosophy could make for a very bad political philosophy.[19] An unpublished postscript to OGG sheds light on her thinking.[20] In the original essay, Murdoch speaks of the need for a moral philosophy "out of which aesthetic and political views can be generated" (OGG: 46). She then goes on to say a great deal about ethics in relation to art and almost nothing about its relation to politics. In the postscript she explains that morality and politics – unlike (in her view) morality and aesthetics – "can never quite form a single system." She continues:

> Any serious moral viewpoint is likely to imply at least one political axiom. But if the axiom implied is the axiom of individual freedom, this in itself effects a certain severance between morals and politics, which may make it improper to use the same images [pictures] in both fields. (For instance, one may think it right to coerce oneself into being good, but not right to coerce another into being good). The idea of excellence has then a different operation in morals from its operation in politics, since a final acceptance of

---

[17] Murdoch writes: "[W]hen we leave the domain of the purely logical we come into the cloudy and shifting domain of the concepts which men live by – and these are subject to historical change. This is especially true of moral concepts" (ME: 74–75). Hämäläinen 2022 and Browning 2019 and 2018b emphasize this aspect of Murdoch's view.

[18] Blum points particularly to "A House of Theory," where Murdoch discusses "a loss of energy" in the socialist movement in Britain and refers to political philosophy as a "department of ethics" (177). This 1958 essay, in which Murdoch identifies as a socialist, contains much that is of interest. For discussion see Browning 2024, 2018a: 121–123; Jamieson 2023: ch. 6; Blum 2022b: 424–427.

[19] And vice-versa: "Good political philosophy is not necessarily good moral philosophy" (SGC: 78–79).

[20] PSP (2011 [1966]).

> imperfection and incompleteness is built into politics in a way in which it is not built into personal morals. The command "Be perfect," which can never do harm to the artist or the moral agent, is a very dangerous political slogan (PSP: 6).[21]

In this rich passage, Murdoch expresses reservations about transferring concepts from her moral philosophy to the political domain. We need, then, to be careful about making this kind of move. At the same time, we need to be careful not to posit too sharp a separation between the moral and the political. There is, after all, a clear commonsense connection between the two. And there are three additional reasons to allow for such a connection.

First, Murdoch considered it an essential feature of morality that it could not be neatly segregated from other areas of life or study.[22]

Second, Murdoch insists on the necessity of bringing moral standards to bear on politics, and she takes it that doing so is perfectly compatible with political liberalism.[23]

Third, even in MGM, where Murdoch is most cautious about mixing ethics and politics, she recognizes vital connections between them. She maintains, for instance, that the modern democratic state depends for its survival on "an atmosphere of moral good will and high ideals" and that our political and moral lives constantly – and often properly – intermingle, "as when we argue about pornography, pacifism, abortion, medicine and hundreds of topics which are in the newspapers every day" (MGM: 362–363 and ch. 12, *passim*; MGM: 358). For Murdoch, "morality enters politics in an unsystematic way," but it enters it (MGM: 378). She affirms their interconnection in the very passage

---

[21] Murdoch distinguishes similarly between moral and political conceptions of freedom in a contemporaneous essay (DPR: 201).

[22] "It is a peculiarity of ethics that the initial segregation of the items to be studied is less easy than in other branches of philosophy" (VC: 32/76). Murdoch's own view was that morals and moral philosophy properly concern "the whole of our mode of living and the quality of our relations with the world" (SGC: 95). She believed, further, that one's picture of morality – whatever it might be – expresses one's moral attitudes (VC: 58/98).

[23] "We are accustomed to say: morality is a private business, it concerns what goes on in a man's soul, while politics is a matter of external expediency and arrangements. And this point of view, which is roughly the liberal democratic point of view, is of course a healthy one in that it suggests that it is not the duty of the government to interfere with people's minds, or to try to make them good .... Indeed, it is just this point of view which most of all distinguishes our form of government from a totalitarian one" (MB: 22–23). Yet, Murdoch goes on to say, it also makes it difficult to think about the politics of nuclear armament. She concludes that what is needed is a new way to bring the "decent, sensible morality of ordinary people all over the world" to bear on politics (25). In "Political Morality and the War in Vietnam," which appeared one year *after* Murdoch wrote the postscript to OGG, Murdoch again stresses the necessity of treating political decisions as moral decisions and the possibility of doing this in a way that is both realistic and liberal in spirit: "The Vietnamese are fighting a just war against the Americans. This vocabulary almost sounds old-fashioned. But let us keep alive the possibility of making such distinctions" (PM: 8).

from the postscript in which she calls for their separation. It is precisely the commitment to individual freedom that Murdoch sees as necessitating "a certain severance" between morality and politics. "*If* the axiom implied is the axiom of individual freedom ... this in itself effects a certain severance ...." Murdoch here affirms the antecedent of the conditional and treats it as the implication of a moral viewpoint.

Given these considerations, it seems best that any political significance we attach to Murdoch's concept of the individual be sensitive to the value of individual freedom.[24] Accordingly, I assign to the concept a purely informal role in supporting the liberal spirit and in nourishing thereby "the atmosphere" that makes liberal democracy possible. I do not treat this concept as the basis for institutional design or government policy. This minimizes the possibility that it could be used coercively.

That leaves difficulty (1b): the possibility of conflating different concepts of the individual or different periods in Murdoch's thinking. To lessen this possibility, and to keep things manageable, I limit myself in this work to discussing Murdoch's early and middle writings.[25]

1.6 Preview

There are other reasons for restricting the scope of my inquiry in this way. Murdoch's bold and brilliant early writings have received comparatively little scholarly attention.[26] Reading them together with the writings from her middle period helps us to appreciate both what was initially present in Murdoch's thinking and what emerged subsequently in *The Sovereignty of Good*. Doing so should also help us better to appreciate what is specific to Murdoch's later writings.

I proceed by tracing different paths from Murdoch's concept of the individual to the liberal spirit. In Section 2 I show how Murdoch develops a "naturalistic" frame or background for the individual agent that primes him to experience the value of other persons without slighting or subordinating his own value. In Sections 3 and 4 I move within this frame to examine three features of Murdoch's "naturalized" individual: his uniqueness, his transcendence, and his dependence on the exercise of love to reach a knowledge of others or to be known by others. The aim is to illuminate the affinities between Murdoch's

---

[24] Cf. Sanchez-Schilling 2019.
[25] Rather than treating the concept of the individual in *Sovereignty* as a distinct alternative to the concept that Muroch develops in her early writings, I proceed on the assumption that the essays in *Sovereignty* enrich the earlier concept. My discussion should help to show the plausibility of this assumption.
[26] With the very valuable exception of Jamieson 2023.

picture of the individual and the ideal of a society in which human beings live together as free equals.[27]

2 The Individual and Her Background

[T]o try to understand the animal apart from its background ... is to risk the collapse of both. To be what they are they require each other.[28]

2.1 Introduction

Tony Bennett was once asked whether Ella Fitzgerald ever talked about the epic hostility directed at American Blacks in their own country. He replied: "She never made a political statement ... except when I heard her say three words .... She said, 'Tony, we're all here'" (Woodhead 2019). An evocative comment – but where is *here*? We can think of Murdoch's first published papers in moral philosophy as comparing two ways to conceptualize the "here" in which humans are placed, corresponding to what Murdoch calls the "liberal" and "naturalistic" outlooks.[29] Murdoch takes these outlooks both to shape and to reflect the moral thinking of ordinary people in the West, as well as philosophical theories of morality and mind. They represent, in her words, "total differences of moral vision and perspective" (ME: 71).[30] In this section I sketch these two outlooks, consider Murdoch's reasons for thinking the liberal outlook to be inadequate to Enlightenment ideals of the liberal world, and show how she adumbrates a modified version of the naturalistic outlook to offset the liberal outlook's deficiencies.

2.2 The Naturalistic and Liberal Outlooks

On what Murdoch calls the *naturalistic* outlook, morality is seen as continuous with "some sort of larger structure of reality," which may be religious, social or

---

[27] Following Murdoch's lead, I focus my discussion on *human* individuals, though it is an important and (to me) attractive feature of Murdoch's concept of the individual that its application is not restricted to human beings. My analysis will naturally raise questions about the extent to which the features I examine in Sections 3 and 4 are shared by, or apply to our relations with, non-human individuals. Although I will not be addressing these issues here, I hope that my inquiry helps to make them more tractable. See Milligan 2022.

[28] Lopez 2001: 177.

[29] Murdoch speaks of the "Natural Law" outlook in ME and of the "naturalistic" outlook in VC. I take her to be exploring the same type of outlook in the two papers and refer to it as "naturalistic." Murdoch uses the terms "naturalism" and "naturalist" to mean, very roughly, what we mean by moral realism and moral realist (Broackes 2012: 16).

[30] Murdoch puts these models forward as ideal-types. While her emphasis is on the fact that different people may (and do) hold radically different pictures of morality, she notes that the same individual may hold, or use, different pictures at different times (ME: 70; VC: 57/97). I return to this point in 2.8.

historical, and which both "contains" and "transcends" the individual agent (ME: 65). The Marxist, for instance, understands morality in terms of a wider historical process that includes distinct stages of class struggle and culminates in a genuinely communist form of society. The Christian views it in relation to the ultimate reality of the Christian God. Murdoch stresses that one who holds a naturalistic outlook (the "naturalist") sees fact and value as joined in important ways; he sees his conception of how to live as connected to, or implicit in, certain facts about the world.[31] In Murdoch's words:

> The individual is seen as moving tentatively vis-à-vis a reality which transcends him. To discover what is morally good is to discover that reality, and to become good is to integrate himself with it (ME: 60).

Importantly, for the naturalist, some of these facts are elusive or hard to reach. What is more, "freedom" for the naturalist is connected to increasing one's understanding of these essential and elusive facts. Such gains in understanding may have practical force. Murdoch continues:

> [The individual] is ruled by laws which he can only partly understand. He is not fully conscious of what he is. His freedom is not an open freedom of choice in a clear situation; it lies rather in an increasing knowledge of his own real being, and in the conduct which naturally springs from such knowledge (ME: 60).

I'd like to represent the naturalistic outlook in terms of four interdependent postulates. This is an expository device. The postulates capture the main commitments of the naturalistic outlook, as Murdoch conceives it, and they will be useful to refer to going forward:

(1N) Morality is part of a larger structure or reality that transcends the agent; it presupposes a transcendent background to the individual.
(2N) Fact and value are interlinked; value is a genuine part of the world or universe.
(3N) Freedom originates in knowledge of self and world; such knowledge is necessarily partial and possesses practical force.
(4N) Moral activity may be purely inward; it need not issue in observable behavior.

By contrast, Murdoch associates what she calls the *liberal* outlook with the attempt to eliminate metaphysics and psychology from ethics.[32] In Murdoch's words:

---

[31] "The Marxist regards his analysis, with its key concepts such as the dialectic, the role of the proletariat, and so on, as recording objective facts about the nature of the universe" (EH: 111).
[32] I say "attempt" because Murdoch argues that the outlook is merely *unconscious of* its metaphysical and psychological commitments.

> Morality [on the liberal outlook] is not explained in terms of metaphysical concepts ... nor in terms of psychological concepts ..... It is not pictured ... as being attached to any real natural or metaphysical structure. It is pictured without any transcendent background. It is presented simply in terms of exhortations and choices defended by reference to facts (ME: 63).

The image here is that of an individual who inhabits a straightforwardly empirical world. The individual introduces value into this world through his choices and in so doing he exercises his freedom.

> [W]e picture the individual as able to attain by reflection to complete consciousness of his situation. He is entirely free to choose and responsible for his choice. His morality is exhibited in his choice, whereby he shows which things he regards as valuable (ME: 70).

The liberal outlook *mirrors* that of the naturalistic outlook. It can be thought of in terms of the four postulates that I introduced above, but (roughly) inverted. This, again, is an expository device that will prove useful. According to the liberal outlook:

(1L) Morality precludes the idea of a reality that transcends the individual; there is no transcendent background to the agent.

(2L) Fact and value are entirely separate; value is a product of the will, not a genuine part of the world.

(3L) Freedom consists in choosing for oneself how to connect facts to values; the facts are wholly available to any rational observer and motivationally inert.

(4L) Moral activity is perforce observable; a person's morality is (purely) a matter of outward actions.

Although Murdoch views both outlooks as originating in Kant, there is an important sense in which they are not equally modern.[33] The naturalistic outlook takes up Kant's commitment to a transcendent background to moral life, to something above and beyond the will of the individual.[34] The liberal outlook takes up Kant's commitment to securing the individual's autonomy by excluding value from the world (and locating it in the will).[35] It is the second idea, not the first, that is quintessentially "modern," in the sense of belonging to the Enlightenment. We can say, then, that the liberal outlook represents for

---

[33] "Kant himself is the source not only of this Liberal morality, but also of a modern version of its opposite" (ME: 68).

[34] "Kant's man lives in a universe where there is a transcendent objective truth, although it may not be altogether knowable" (EPM: 134). Murdoch considers Kant a metaphysical naturalist.

[35] The liberal outlook is *neo*-Kantian. It is Kant's view stripped of his belief in a priori principles of reason. Murdoch views the liberal outlook as arising from an amalgamation of Kant and Hume.

Murdoch the Enlightenment (or *officially* modern) worldview and the naturalistic outlook represents the modern face of a premodern worldview.

2.3 The Naturalistic Outlook and the Liberal Spirit

Given this, one might expect the liberal *outlook* to support the liberal *sensibility* (or "spirit"), that is, the disposition to regard others as "having a right to exist and to have a separate mode of being which is important and interesting to themselves" (SBR: 257/271). This is, after all, an Enlightenment ideal, perhaps *the* Enlightenment ideal. One would expect the Enlightenment worldview to serve or support Enlightenment ideals. As we will see, the liberal outlook does indeed support the liberal sensibility, in Murdoch's view, but only to a point. To locate that point, it will be helpful to look first at the naturalistic outlook and the degree to which *it* supports a liberal sensibility.

Let's start by taking a closer look at the first postulate of the naturalistic outlook.

(1N) Morality is part of a larger structure or reality that transcends the agent; it presupposes a transcendent background to the individual.

The OED tells us that "transcend" can be traced back to the Latin term *tran(s) scendĕre*, meaning to climb over or beyond, to surmount or surpass. What does it mean to say that a background transcends the agent? What does Murdoch mean by this?

On the reading presented here, Murdoch's analyses in ME and VC provide us with importantly different answers to this question. In this section I'll focus on ME, the earlier of the two papers. I'll turn to VC, and spell out the relevant difference, in 2.9.[36]

In ME, the naturalist assigns more importance – categorically more importance – to the background structure than to the individual. In Murdoch's words:

> The individual is seen as held in a framework which transcends him, where what is important and valuable is the framework, and the individual only has importance, or even reality, in so far as he belongs to the framework (ME: 70).

Murdoch continues (returning to a passage I quoted in 2.2):

> Here the individual is seen as moving tentatively vis-à-vis a reality which transcends him. To discover what is morally good is to discover that reality, and to become good is to integrate himself with it (ME: 70).

---

[36] "Metaphysics and Ethics" was published in 1957, one year after "Vision and Choice in Morality," but delivered as a BBC talk in 1955 (Broackes 2012: 23). I therefore consider it the earlier paper despite its later publication date. Thanks to Anil Gomes for help with these details.

This is a picture in which the background reality transcends the individual in a *hierarchical* sense, in the sense of *endowing her with value* (and so, by implication, surpassing her in value). Again: "[W]hat is important and valuable is the framework, and the individual only has importance, or even reality, in so far as he belongs to the framework" (70). Here the framework confers value on the individual; the individual's value is conditional on, and subordinate to, the framework's value. In short, ME offers us a hierarchical way of interpreting the idea of a transcendent background, a hierarchical version of the naturalistic outlook.

Hierarchical naturalism (as I shall call it) can be developed in different ways, as Murdoch's grouping together of Thomists with Marxists and Hegelians suggests (ME: 70). It is, if you like, a *species* (hierarchical) of a *genus* (naturalistic) of moral outlook. It has a notable affinity, however, with premodern ideals of social or political order, wherein the individual properly derives her standing and identity from her position in an authoritative and pre-existing hierarchy (e.g., caste, feudal, patriarchal). It is good to remember that hierarchical forms of society were the norm in the West prior to the Enlightenment, and to appreciate that they continue to appeal to a great many people. Hierarchically ordered societies have the potential to furnish individuals with a stable sense of identity, purpose, and connection by linking those things to a wider natural or metaphysical framework.[37]

Hierarchical naturalism is not consistent with, nor is it meant to be consistent with, a liberal sensibility. For the hierarchical naturalist, as we have seen, the individual has no value (or even being) apart from the whole. The background reality is the source of the individual's value. Should it require the sacrifice of one's life, as God demanded the sacrifice of Isaac's life, or of one's agency, as patriarchal societies often demand of women, there is no question within this outlook of what, in principle, one ought to do. To put it plainly, individuals per se are not important to the hierarchical naturalist; they derive their value from the *whole*.

This way of thinking can be, and has been, deployed to sanction systems of gross exploitation, but it need not be so used.[38] The core idea can be seen in Bessie Head's story, "The Lovers" (1990). The protagonists, Keaja and Tselane, belong to a village that follows traditional ways of life that are (thought to be) patterned on the cosmological order; to violate these traditional mores is to rupture this order and thereby to imperil the community. Strictly prearranged

---

[37] See generally Hahn 2024; Wilkerson 2020; Dumont 1986, 1980.
[38] Christian defenders of American chattel slavery, for instance, appealed to this way of thinking. As Jones explains: "Like a symbiotic ecosystem, genders and races had their roles to play, and when all parts functioned as designed, the ecosystem thrived and individual members – whatever their lots – were [allegedly] content, since they were fulfilling their created purpose" (2021: 82).

and "emotionally sterile" marriages form a critical part of the traditional ways. Any personal unhappiness that might arise from such marriages passes quickly (or ought to); daily life in the community is peaceful and harmonious. Keaja's family has already planned a marriage for him when he and Tselane – who is not his appointed marriage partner – fall deeply in love and feel compelled to marry one another. Because they were brought up within a hierarchical naturalistic outlook, they struggle in a very fundamental way to make sense of their situation. As Tselane tells Keaja:

> My training has told me that people are not important in themselves but you so suddenly became important to me, as a person. I did not know how to tell my mother all this yet she was kind and took care of me. Eventually I thought I would lose my mind (1990: 96).

Murdoch neither endorses nor rejects hierarchical naturalism in ME (or VC). In these papers, her chief concern was to argue that philosophers should not dismiss views of this sort simply because they appeal to transcendent entities or "metaphysics." In addition, she was concerned to show that the liberal outlook was just that, an outlook on morality – albeit an outlook that came naturally to members of postwar Britain.[39] Murdoch argued that the failure of philosophers who operated within this outlook to see it as such – as one possible outlook among others – had led them to neglect the variety of moral thought and, in particular, the importance to much moral thinking of a belief in something that transcends the individual. But in a roughly contemporaneous piece that Murdoch published on T.S. Eliot, she rejects hierarchical naturalism precisely for its devaluation of the individual. It is worth quoting her at length:

> It seems to me that Mr Eliot plays dangerously when he rejects *in toto* the moral content of liberalism and appeals over its head to a conception of dogma and authority which can itself play an ambivalent role . . . . To argue in this way is to belittle that naked respect for the human person as such which one may connect with Locke and with Kant, and which one hopes has become a part of the English political tradition. Can this be set aside as a romantic over-valuation of the individual? It is at least perilous to neglect the remnants of that liberal moral absolutism which, without dogma, holds that there are certain things which cannot be done to human persons . . . . It may be that the Christian tradition must be the salvation of the West; but to argue this too narrowly is to neglect aspects of liberalism which are, to put it mildly, worth preserving . . . . But whatever our religious beliefs, we must hope that the liberal world can regenerate itself out of its own resources – and we must seek

---

[39] "This is only one type of view of morality – roughly a Protestant; and less roughly a Liberal, type of view" (ME: 68); "I have wished to deny the claim of the current view to picture morality as such. The current view pictures a type of morality" (VC: 57).

the Christian tradition, in its various forms, within that world . . . . to say this is, of course, to take up a liberal attitude (TSM: 168; also SBR: 259–264/273–278).

In this rich passage we see Murdoch's embrace of the Enlightenment ideal of "respect for the human person as such" and her identification with a liberal sensibility (or "attitude").[40] "[T]here are certain things which cannot be done to human persons" – for any reason, Murdoch implies, because the individual is precious, and because the individual should be permitted to live the life that she desires, provided that she allows others to do the same. Murdoch considers these ideals to be "aspects of liberalism" well worth preserving, and she rejects hierarchical naturalism because it does not and cannot support them.

2.4 The Liberal Outlook and the Liberal Spirit: Part One

Let's turn now to consider how well the liberal outlook supports a liberal sensibility. This is more complicated and will occupy us for the next five sections (2.4–2.8). As before, I'll approach this matter through what I have characterized as the first postulate of this outlook.

(1L) Morality precludes the idea of a reality that transcends the individual; there is no transcendent background to the agent.

In considering this postulate, it is helpful to note that Murdoch distinguishes two philosophical versions of the liberal outlook in her early work.[41] First, what might be called the Francophone or Sartrean "existentialist" version, which dismisses the notion of any substantial (natural or metaphysical) background to morality. It pictures the individual as making choices in a complete vacuum. There are plain empirical facts on one side and values on the other and no connective tissue – no social, rational or other natural or metaphysical "structure" (such as religion) – linking the two. Discussing Sartre's *Being and Nothingness*, Murdoch presents the view this way:

> Are we accepting too readily the standards of our society or of our church? Is our picture of the world distorted by an unwillingness to face unpleasant facts about ourselves? These questions are asked in the context of a fundamental loneliness of the individual, where there is no answer to the questioning except a decision, an affirmation of meaning the objectivity of which nothing certifies. We ask: Is what we value really valuable? We must answer – and yet this cannot be in terms of objective values, for there are none (NM:105).

---

[40] We see this attitude implicitly at work in Murdoch's thoughtful defense of same-sex relationships in "The Moral Decision About Homosexuality" (1964). Cf. Lovibond 2011 and note 4 above.

[41] SBR: 249–255/264–270; AD: 287–289. By the time of *Sovereignty* Murdoch treats them as different "wings" of existentialism: the "Continental" or "Surrealist" and the "Anglo-Saxon" or "Kantian" (IP: 26, 34).

Things look a bit different according to what might be called the Anglophone or empiricist version of the liberal outlook (SBR: 253–256/264–270).[42] Here there *is* a notable background to morality; it consists in the network of ordinary language and the ordinary reasoning that the agent uses to formulate and communicate his choices. On this picture, the agent surveys the facts and then connects them to evaluative properties, whose valence is fixed by the common language, based on his principles. The principles are his to choose, but he is answerable to others for the accuracy of his factual survey or for the consistency of his choices relative to his chosen principles (Jamieson 2023: 123–131). The ordinary language and ordinary forms of reasoning supply the agent with a shared (and social) background and a common currency with which to formulate and reflect on his choices.

Nevertheless, Murdoch stresses, the empiricist agent faces the same basic predicament as the existentialist agent: choosing how to act in a world that cannot itself sanction one's choices. The world cannot sanction the empiricist agent's choices any more than it can sanction the existentialist agent's choices because, by 2L (according to which fact and value are entirely separate), the world is not a source of value; we bring value to it. Murdoch connects 2L to the view, now known as scientism, that the world contains only what falls under the purview of the natural sciences; by these lights, the world is *unable* to contain any value properties.[43]

But now one might wonder why, on the liberal outlook, the world can't be said to transcend the agent. After all, the world that is revealed by the natural sciences is truly impressive – in its magnitude, in its complexity and, of course, in its importance to human life. It is certainly "greater than" than any one individual; individuals, after all, depend upon *it*. One might wonder, then, why it can't be said to transcend the individual. This is to ask, in short, why 1L is essential to the liberal outlook and how exactly to understand this postulate.

Earlier, in discussing hierarchical naturalism, we isolated one way for a background to transcend the agent – by conferring importance on him: "What is important and valuable is the framework, and the individual only has importance, or even reality, in so far as he belongs to the framework" (ME: 70). The world as it is known through science, however, does not look like a good candidate for this kind of transcendence. While many religions and

---

[42] Murdoch associates this version with different philosophers, depending on her concerns. In SBR, whose argument focuses on literature, she associates it with Stevenson; in ME and VC, which focus on moral philosophy, with Hare; and in AD, which also focuses on literature, with Hampshire.

[43] It is not science that is the problem for Murdoch but rather "the domination of inexact ideas of science" (IP: 26).

cultures worship the natural world and see it as value-conferring, what they're worshipping is not the natural world as conceived by science. Still, one might wonder, isn't there some other morally relevant (and less draconian) way for the world to transcend the agent on the liberal outlook?

The answer to this question, on Murdoch's account, has to be "no," because the stipulated absence of value in the world (2L) precludes any constituents of the world from having moral relevance, and because this absence is essential to the outlook. On the liberal worldview, "however grandiose the structure may be ... the moral agent is responsible for endowing the totality with value" (ME: 71).[44] The background *must* leave the question of value wide open because only then, by 3L (which identifies freedom with untrammeled choice), can we think of the individual's will as autonomous. As Murdoch (later) puts it: "if the will is to be totally free the world it moves in must be devoid of normative characteristics" (IP: 40).[45]

The lesson here is twofold. First, the ultimate background to the agent on the liberal outlook, the "here" in which she moves, is a morally empty and inert world. Second, in such a world, there is nothing to transcend the agent in a morally significant way, whether by according her importance or by properly conditioning what she cares about and what she chooses. This is the significance of 1L.

2.5 The Liberal Outlook and the Liberal Spirit: Part Two

Murdoch thinks that the liberal outlook's conception of the individual's background goes with a picture of the individual *herself* that is unwittingly "romantic." On the liberal outlook, there is nothing in the world to seriously challenge or compel the self: there is just the self with its chosen concerns, confronting a world that is (taken to be) devoid of value. It thus invites a kind of romantic bravado.[46]

---

[44] This applies to the empiricist version of the outlook despite its recognition of a socio-linguistic background to the agent. Murdoch says: "Ordinary Language Man ... is not overwhelmed by any structure larger than himself, such as might be represented by a metaphysical belief or by an institution. As a moral agent he is completely free, choosing between acts and reasons on his own responsibility" (SBR: 254/268). Accordingly, ordinary language *itself* is taken to be something the agent uses to express her values; it is merely a tool, "an instrument of commendation" (SBR: 253/268).

[45] "Good must be thought of, not as part of the world, but as a moveable label affixed to the world; for only so can the agent be pictured as responsible and free" (IP: 4).

[46] Lipscomb 2022 describes the kind of bravado Murdoch might have in mind: "[A] self-congratulatory toughness in facing a world where the words 'God' and 'Good' have no meaning" (43); "The world is cold, pitiless, bereft. But however grim it sounds ... there is exaltation in beholding the bleakness of it all, or in having steeled oneself to look without flinching" (19). Murdoch also uses the term romantic (capitalized) in a narrower historical sense connected to Hegel. See Antonaccio 2000: 100–107.

Murdoch sees the liberal outlook's romantic picture of the individual as something that may work with, as well as against, a liberal sensibility. Let's consider first how it can support a liberal sensibility.

In a remarkable passage in SGC, Murdoch likens the romantic individual to Milton's Lucifer (!) and yet deems him both "the ideal citizen of the liberal state, a warning held up to tyrants," and the inspiration of political liberalism (SGC: 78–79).[47] We could read this as a withering condemnation of liberalism *tout court*, but this would be to oversimplify. Murdoch is registering that despite its rather serious failings, this picture of the individual also embodies the Enlightenment ideals that she cherishes.

Murdoch doesn't spell out how she sees the romantic individual as embodying or supporting these ideals, but here is one distinct possibility. This picture *liberates* the individual from the structures of external authority that had, historically, been sources of oppression (most obviously religion). The liberal outlook views every individual, rich or poor, Protestant or atheist, as a source and arbiter of value. It precludes any framework or authority to which he should defer or from which his value derives. No transcendent realities "such as God, or History, or the Church" are allowed "to overshadow the moral life" (VC: 55/95). Nor are they allowed to overshadow, or outshine, the individual. The liberal worldview not only permits Keaja and Tselane to recognize each other's importance independently of the socio-cosmological order, it enjoins them to do so. It plainly expresses the idea of the individual as valuable per se. This, we could say, is a dividend of 1L (which rejects a transcendent background to the individual).

Relatedly, the liberal worldview seems to encourage tolerance because it disallows one who holds it from regarding her own morality as a kind of fact about the world or universe (ME: 66). In other words, a dividend of 2L (which separates fact from value) is that one cannot make one's values out to be compulsory for others on the grounds that they follow from "the way things are."[48] Accordingly, the romantic individual will seek to live and let live,

---

[47] The reference to Milton's Lucifer – who would rather reign in hell than serve in heaven – is pointed and appears elsewhere in *Sovereignty* (OGG: 47, 70; SGC: 80, 100; *Paradise Lost*, I. 263).

[48] "Now I suggest there is another type of answer to the question, why not attach morality to the substance of the world? – and that is a moral answer. If you do this you are in danger of making your morality into a dogma, you are in danger of becoming intolerant of the values of others, and of ceasing to reflect on your own values through taking them too much for granted. In short, if you start to think of morality as part of a general way of conceiving the universe, as part of a larger conceptual framework, you may cease to be reflective and responsible about it, you may begin to regard it as a sort of fact. And as soon as you regard your moral system as a sort of fact, and not as a set of values which only exist through your own choices, your moral conduct will degenerate" (ME: 66). However, we should note, Murdoch associates this line of thinking with "the propaganda of Liberalism," so it's not *clear* that Murdoch is speaking for herself in the quoted passage rather than for philosophers who (she believes) have uncritically embraced the

provided that others do the same, because he recognizes that his own way of doing things is just that. In short, he will neither claim undue authority for himself nor suffer it from others. He would thus seem to be "the ideal citizen of the liberal state, a warning held up to tyrants."

It is more difficult to see how the liberal outlook and its romantic picture of the individual might work against the liberal sensibility (or "spirit"). In considering this, I take my lead from remarks that Murdoch makes in her essay "Against Dryness":

> It is natural that a Liberal democratic society will ... emphasise choice .... For political purposes we have been encouraged to think of ourselves as totally free and responsible, knowing everything we need to know for the important purposes of life. But this is one of the things of which Hume said that it may be true in politics but false in fact. And is it really true in politics? We need a post-Kantian unromantic Liberalism with a different image of freedom (AD: 293; also SBR: 270/284).

A few passages later, after noting the dearth of convincing pictures of evil in contemporary literature, Murdoch continues this thought as follows:

> Our inability to imagine evil is a consequence of the facile, dramatic and, in spite of Hitler, optimistic picture of ourselves with which we work .... We need to turn our attention away from ... Romanticism, away from the dry symbol, the bogus individual, the false whole, towards the real impenetrable human person. That this person is substantial, impenetrable, individual, indefinable, and valuable is after all the fundamental tenet of Liberalism (AD: 294).

So: Murdoch sees the romantic individual as both the ideal citizen of the liberal state and, at the same time, as somehow in tension with what she takes to be liberalism's "fundamental tenet." And she takes that tenet to be the belief that persons are substantial, distinct, impenetrable, and indefinable – *as well as* important in their own right. As we will see, this is the very belief that her own conception of the individual is meant to capture. But this is to get ahead. In the next section I show why Murdoch thinks the heroic romantic individual envisaged by the liberal outlook turns out to be weirdly *in*substantial. In 2.7 I then sketch how Murdoch links this cipher-like image of the individual to attitudes that are conducive to intolerance. Finally, in 2.8, I consider how to fit together the relevant strengths and weaknesses of the liberal outlook's romantic picture of the individual.

---

liberal outlook. Jamieson suggests that, for Murdoch, liberal ideas become liberal *propaganda* when they exclude rival views from consideration (2023: 153–161).

2.6 The Liberal Outlook and the Liberal Spirit: Part Three

The liberal outlook identifies the agent's freedom with the ability to confer value in a way that is wholly unconstrained. In this way it aims to guarantee the authenticity of the agent's choices, to ensure that they are truly *his*. This is the force of 3L. Murdoch points out that to secure this type of freedom, the outlook *isolates* the part of the agent that chooses. It identifies the agent with his will, that is, and then quarantines the will in order to ensure that it is not influenced by forces outside of its control. On the one hand, the will is isolated from other aspects of (what we ordinarily call) the agent's self: "immense care is taken to picture the will as isolated. It is isolated from belief, from reason, from feeling, and yet the essential center of the self" (IP: 8). On the other, it is isolated from its material surroundings: there can be, as we saw, nothing in the world to compel it. "If the will is to be ... free the world it moves in must be devoid of normative characteristics" (IP: 40).

In short: the self is reduced to will, the will is sealed off from the world and from other parts of the self, and value is removed from the world. Murdoch was struck by the way that this combination (reduction, isolation, removal) ends up depriving the individual of vital substance and individuality, even as it attributes to him god-like powers. The romantic individual, for all his self-emphasis and because of it, turns out to be a "solitary and substanceless" being, nothing like a distinctive locus of experience with a rich history of perception and thought (IP: 16). Nothing, that is, like an actual person or self. Such a figure, Murdoch notes, is scarcely recognizable as an agent. One who sees herself as an isolated will can't see her choices as warranted by anything in the world or as expressive of her vision of objective reality. Is she really even choosing then? "If we are so strangely separate from the world at moments of choice are we really choosing at all, are we right indeed to identify *ourselves* with this giddy empty will?" (IP: 35).[49]

Instead of presenting us, then, with a life-like agent in a life-like world, the liberal outlook presents us with "a brave naked will surrounded by an easily comprehended empirical world" (AD: 290). Murdoch wants us to see that these simplified notions of self and world complement each other. For the world to be easily comprehended, the individuals populating it must themselves be easily comprehended: free of internal depths, readily compassed. And, correspondingly, to view people in this way, the world in which they make their choices must be morally inert and simple. But in such a world – coming full circle, now – there is little to occasion the kind of inner life we associate with persons or agency. The figure suggested by such a background is neither substantial nor

---

[49] For an inspired development of the idea that we must see our desires as responses to properties in the world if we are to have genuine agency, see Bilgrami 2014: ch. 5.

distinctive nor in any way out of reach. This, we could say, is the price of freedom as it is construed by 3L: identifying freedom with choosing one's values, it leaves no one to do the choosing.[50]

Murdoch criticizes this reductive picture of the self (and its world) on various grounds. Our concern is with how she sees it as itself working against the liberal spirit, against a readiness to see others as having their own valid paths in life, however different those paths might be from one's own.

2.7 The Liberal Outlook and the Liberal Spirit: Part Four

Murdoch's comments on this point are more suggestive than explicit. However, they point in a certain direction that we could summarize in this way: one who pictures herself as a "solitary, substanceless" chooser in a morally simple world is not poised to take an interest in the lives of others or to be modest about her own grasp of things, and – Murdoch thinks – a person must possess both of these qualities if she is to be reliably tolerant of others and respectful of human difference.[51] In Murdoch's words, the liberal outlook fails to provide its possessor with "a stand-point for considering real human beings in their variety" or "any technique for exploring and controlling our own spiritual energy" in relation to others (SBR: 255). Similarly: "A simple-minded faith in science, together with the assumption that we are all rational and free, engenders a dangerous lack of curiosity about the real world, a failure to appreciate the difficulties of knowing it" (AD: 293).

The concepts of convention and neurosis, which correspond to the Anglophone and Francophone versions of the liberal outlook discussed in 2.4, help to articulate Murdoch's thinking in this connection. Very roughly, these designate pathologies that Murdoch associates with the liberal conception of the individual (S&G: 215–218; SBR: 254–255/268–270). With "convention," Murdoch is not targeting conventional understandings or mores per se; she is targeting excessive reliance on conventional ways of thinking, that is, "groupthink." She suggests that one who is guided by the liberal picture of the individual in its Anglophone version will be susceptible to groupthink because, lacking a sense of the rich inner life that distinguishes individuals from one another, he will too readily trust in "the network of moral conceptual activity at its most common and universally

---

[50] The more general idea is that how we conceive of persons conditions how we conceive of the world and vice-versa. Gomes 2025 uses this idea to illuminate Murdoch's argument in IP.

[51] Jamieson 2023: 168–177. On Jamieson's analysis, Murdoch connects a belief in the transcendent to practices of critical reflection.

accepted level" to provide a suitable standard or medium for thinking about other persons (SBR: 254/268).[52]

"Neurosis" indicates a condition of anxious self-absorption that Murdoch associates with the Francophone (or Sartrean) version of the liberal outlook. The neurotic becomes wrapped up in *angst* over his radical freedom, his need to make decisions, while lacking any objective basis for what he decides. He is thus drawn into hyper-reflection in lieu of a properly engaged consideration of the world and people around him; he closes in on himself since (by his lights) there is nothing in the world to ground his values (SBR: 254–255/268–270; also S&G: 216; Holland 2012). Murdoch sees neurosis and convention as mutually reinforcing conditions (SBR: 254/268). Absent the sense of a rich inner or outer world, she suggests, efforts to break out of self-absorption (should they occur!) lead one to conventional views and vice-versa. Both conditions make it hard, or impossible, for one to grasp what Murdoch calls "the reality" of other persons/individuals.[53] What does this mean?

Murdoch associates the reality of persons with their importance, their substantiality, and their difference (e.g., SBR: 261/275; HMD: 149). These are all qualities, we should note, that figure in her description of liberalism's chief tenet. The concept of an individual's reality highlights the gap, or distance, between what one sees when one regards another and what is there to be seen. The person in the grip of neurosis or convention is one who is not sufficiently alive to this gap. His problem, on Murdoch's account, is not that he sees others through the prism of conventional or personal categories but that he *reduces* others to what these categories make of them. Murdoch thinks that such a person does not grasp that other persons are *real*.

A passage from Jamaica Kincaid's *Lucy* (1990) might be helpful here. Mariah, for whom the narrator of the novel (Lucy) works as a nanny, is a very warm-hearted person. The two of them have just arrived at the summerhouse that belongs to Mariah's family. Lucy says:

> When we got to our destination, a man Mariah had known all her life, a man who had always done things for her family, a man who came from Sweden, was waiting for us. His name was Gus, and the way Mariah spoke his name it was as if he belonged to her deeply, like a memory. And, of course, he was a part of her past, her childhood: he was there, apparently, when she took

---

[52] One who subscribes to hierarchical naturalism might also be susceptible to convention, albeit for different reasons. See Jamieson's discussion of Murdoch's critique of dogmatic forms of Marxism (Jamieson 2023: 178–184).

[53] E.g., "Wherein does the reality of a person reside and in what way can one, or should one, display that reality?" (SBR: 247/261).

her first steps; she had caught her first fish in a boat with him . . . and so on. Still, he was a real person, and I thought Mariah should have long separated the person Gus standing in front of her in the present from all the things he had meant to her in the past (33–34).

Mariah's view of Gus is deeply affectionate but, if Lucy is right about her, it misses something important.[54] It misses that Gus is not just what he means or has meant to Mariah, that he is necessarily more than (and so at variance with) that. "Still, he was a real person." If Mariah has been afflicted by either convention or neurosis, as Murdoch conceives these, she will persist in this reductive conception of Gus, this obliviousness to his independent reality. And this will attenuate Mariah's sense of his dignity. Should Gus wish to retire from his caretaker job earlier than anticipated, someone in the grip of convention or neurosis might well be unable to see this as anything but betrayal or irresponsibility. Such a person need have no sense that there might be something wrong with the script she is working from, or that there can be no definitive script, that Gus's mode of being is neither the same as hers, nor necessarily congruent with hers, nor fully comprehensible to her, nor hers to decide.

Let me draw together the different points here. Murdoch suggests that one who pictures himself or others as "free choosers in an empirically straightforward world" will be ill-prepared to be tolerant of actual individuals – who turn out be substantial, and various, and who inhabit a morally complicated and challenging world. Such a person will be susceptible to excessively conventional or self-referential ways of thinking, disinclined to approach others with a modicum of curiosity and modesty. Not because he takes himself to have privileged access to the moral truth – as one who holds the naturalistic outlook might – but because he greatly underestimates the complexity of others and of the world as it bears on morality. He isn't well-prepared to recognize "the reality" of other individuals, where this includes their distance from his own ideas of them and from his own way of being in the world. This, Murdoch implies, is not a recipe for tolerance.

2.8 The Liberal Outlook and the Liberal Spirit: Part Five

Stepping back. We've been considering how well the liberal outlook supports the liberal spirit that is the lifeblood of liberal democracy. We noted that the liberal outlook affirms the importance of the individual per se, but also loses sight of the individual's substance and depth. It thus, by Murdoch's lights, works both for and against the liberal sensibility. How are we to fit these opposing tendencies together? Murdoch doesn't exactly tell us. Let me suggest

---

[54] One of the many pleasures of the novel is that it's not clear whether Lucy *is* right about Mariah.

one way to integrate them that follows the lead of Murdoch's remarks but also goes beyond them. I take Murdoch to be inviting the thought that while the liberal outlook's romantic image affirms the absolute value of the individual, it doesn't sufficiently prime us to experience the value of others *in concreto*.[55] One can sincerely endorse the idea that others deserve respect but feel quite differently in their actual presence. This is particularly so in certain situations, such as when one has been conditioned to view members of a certain social group as inferior, or when one is dealing with disorienting cultural changes.

The wider idea is that members of liberal societies need to be able to picture themselves in *more* ways than as monarchs of a disenchanted world. It's as if a picture of the individual fitted to certain contexts overstepped its bounds and threatened to become *the* picture for all contexts.[56] Murdoch thinks that however essential the liberal outlook's romantic picture of the individual might be (or have been) to liberal ideals, it is far from sufficient. It doesn't do justice to what she takes to be the bedrock of liberal democracy: the idea that persons are not only valuable but also substantial, unique, and only partially accessible (AD: 294). She thinks that liberal democracies need a picture of the individual that reflects and reinforces this underlying tenet, that encourages a modicum of curiosity and modesty, and thereby primes us to experience the reality of others.

To conclude this section, I examine Murdoch's own sketch of such a picture. This takes us back to the naturalistic outlook – with a very important modification.

2.9 A Liberal Naturalism

In a memorable passage, Murdoch describes herself and her readers as "heirs of the Enlightenment, Romanticism, and the Liberal tradition" who have not yet recovered from two world wars or the experience of Hitler and who "have been left with far too shallow and flimsy an idea of human personality" (AD: 287). After briefly rehearsing the liberal outlook she says:

> What have we lost here? And what have we perhaps never had? We have suffered a general loss of concepts, the loss of a moral and political vocabulary .... We no longer see man against a background of values, of realities, which transcend him. We picture man as a brave naked will surrounded by an easily comprehended empirical world. For the hard idea of truth we have substituted a facile idea of sincerity. What we have never had ... is a satisfactory Liberal theory of personality, a theory of man as free

---

[55] "We know that the real lesson to be taught is that the human person is precious and unique; but we seem to be unable to set it forth except in terms of ideology and abstraction" (SSR: 148).
[56] "There are different moral pictures which different individuals use or which the same individual may use *at different times*" (VC: 57/97). "*There are times* when it is proper to stress, not the comprehensibility of the world, but its incomprehensibility" (VC: 50/90). Emphases added.

and separate and related to a rich and complicated world from which, as a moral being, he has much to learn. We have bought the Liberal theory as it stands, because we have wished to encourage people to think of themselves as free, at the cost of surrendering the background (AD: 290).

In this exceedingly rich passage, Murdoch sums up what is missing from the liberal picture of the individual "as it stands": a background of values, of realities, that transcend the individual. The liberal picture surrendered such a background, Murdoch observes, to protect the idea of the individual as free. We've examined why Murdoch thinks that this strategy achieves, at best, mixed results. A satisfactory picture, Murdoch maintains, will not choose between the freedom of the individual and the richness of his background. It will provide for both. It will supply the individual with a background that is rich and transcendent while preserving the idea of him as free and separate. To put this a touch paradoxically: an apt "Liberal theory of personality" will be a naturalistic theory, albeit one that fits with liberalism's commitment to the sanctity of the individual.[57] The difficulty is *how* to envisage a background that transcends the individual without eclipsing him, or how to conceive of the naturalistic outlook in a way that is not hierarchical.

I find Murdoch's solution to this difficulty to be both powerful and elegant. It can be broken into two simple ideas. First, the idea that the background to the individual consists (primarily) *in other human individuals* and their relations to one another. Second, the idea that these others transcend the individual in the sense of lying beyond, or exceeding, what he can fully comprehend.

Murdoch drew the first idea from her reading of classic liberal thinkers (she mentions Hobbes, Locke, Hume, Kant, and especially Mill). In this respect, we can see her as attempting to help the liberal world to "regenerate itself out of its own resources" (TSM: 168). These thinkers pictured the individual not as vacuous and alone, she notes, but as surrounded by "a plurality of other persons, who are quite separate and different individuals who have to get along together" (SBR: 251/265–266). Murdoch appreciates the social implications of this picture – it envisages "separate and different individuals," but individuals "who have to get along together," "a plurality" of such persons. But she found nothing in the classical thinkers' conception of this plurality to suggest transcendence. She found their conception of it to be "undynamic and naïve" (SBR: 252).[58] Given Murdoch's rejection of hierarchical naturalism, the

---

[57] Antonaccio and Jamieson develop complementary readings (Antonaccio 2000: 111–112 and 2012: 228–231; Jamieson 2023: 178–185).

[58] Murdoch applies a similar criticism, I think, to the twentieth-century empiricist version of the liberal outlook sketched in 2.4. See note 44. In the case of the classical liberal thinkers, Murdoch attributes this defect to their greater interest in the material world. "The real impetus of the philosophical movement with which Liberalism was connected was not primarily moral or political, it was scientific" (SBR: 252/266).

question thus becomes how to conceptualize the *human* surround in such a way that it transcends the agent without subordinating him. In answer to this question, Murdoch developed what I am calling the second idea. To appreciate this stretch of her thought, we must turn to "Vision and Choice," the sequel to "Metaphysics and Ethics." It is here, I suggest, that we can see an important and neglected difference in their two treatments of the idea of transcendence (2.3).

In ME, as we saw, Murdoch interprets the transcendence of the background hierarchically; the background transcends the agent in that it is the very source of his own value. In VC, Murdoch's language is more ambiguous. On the one hand, she describes the naturalist as one who "*believes* that as moral beings we are immersed in a reality which transcends us and that moral progress consists in awareness of this reality and submission to its purposes" (VC: 56/96). "Submission to its purposes" is, admittedly, about as hierarchical as it gets. But Murdoch's language also points in a different direction when she describes the naturalist as one who "believes that moral values are visions, inspirations or powers which emanate from a transcendent source concerning which he is called on to make discoveries and may at present know little" (VC: 56/96). Her language also points in this alternative direction when, earlier in the paper, she associates the naturalistic model with views "which emphasize the inexhaustible detail of the world, the endlessness of the task of understanding, the importance of not assuming that one has got individuals and situations 'taped,' the connection of knowledge with love and of spiritual insight with apprehension of the unique" (VC: 46/87).[59] She associates these views (and so the naturalistic model) with the belief that "we live in a world whose mystery transcends us and that morality is the exploration of that mystery in so far as it concerns each individual" (VC: 47/88). The language here is less hierarchical than it is perfectionist and mystical. We are invited to think about knowledge in connection with love, about the apprehension of what is unique, about mystery as it concerns the individual, and about the "endlessness of the task of understanding." Readers of Murdoch will recognize this as a pretty good rough description of the view that she will go on to develop in subsequent writings. The point for the moment is that it suggests a different way for morality to have a background that transcends the agent. Instead of the background transcending the agent by endowing her with value – per hierarchical naturalism (and ME) – the background here transcends the agent by surpassing what the agent can fully understand while stirring the agent's desire to understand. That is, the

---

[59] These remarks figure in Murdoch's arguments against identifying moral judgments with universalizable judgments. They are not part of her official description of the naturalistic outlook, then, but by the end of the paper we are able to see the attitude they describe as one possible expression of such an outlook, and as her preferred expression of it.

background transcends the agent not by being *above* her but by being in an important sense *beyond* her. Transcendence in this second sense entails *epistemological distance* as well as some kind of *attraction* to what is distant: "a transcendent source concerning which he is called on to make discoveries" (VC: 56/96). In VC, Murdoch joins this epistemological-erotic sense of transcendence to the empiricist idea that the background to the individual is other individuals who are "quite separate and different" yet connected to one another.

2.10 Liberal Naturalism Developed

In a pair of papers published three years later, in 1959, Murdoch develops this picture in a striking way (S&G; SBR). In these papers, Murdoch likens the plurality of persons to Kant's sublime:

> It is indeed the realization of a vast and varied reality outside ourselves which brings about a sense initially of terror, and when properly understood of exhilaration and spiritual power. But what brings this experience to us, in its most important form, is the sight, not of physical nature, but of our surroundings as consisting of other individual men (SBR: 268/282).

Like Kant's natural (or mathematical) sublime, Murdoch's "human" or "social" sublime both attracts and defeats the individual's efforts to comprehend it. Somewhat more plainly than Kant's sublime, it does this in a way that can be morally transformative.[60] And in keeping with the alternative description of the naturalistic outlook provided in VC, it does not endow the agent with value, though it may well constrain her. It challenges and concentrates her. This is a way of construing the first postulate of the naturalistic outlook (1N) that preserves the individual's unconditional value while supplying him with a morally rich background, one from which the individual "has much to learn."

These papers also elaborate the idea, present but not developed in VC, that it is through *love* that individuals can come to discover or know – never fully – the human "manifold" that surrounds them (S&G: 215–220; SBR: 268–270/282–284; VC: 46/87, 51/91). The addition of this bold idea helps us to see how Murdoch's reworking of the naturalistic outlook joins fact to value and so introduces value into the world (or restores its place there). It is through love (in part) that we come to discover the reality of other people, their actual density

---

[60] As Murdoch later remarks: "Kant's notion of the sublime, though extremely interesting ... is a kind of romanticism. The spectacle of huge and appalling things can indeed exhilarate, but usually in a way that is less than excellent" (OGG: 71). Cf. SBR: 249/263–264. For discussion, see Merritt 2022: esp. 255–257.

and uniqueness, their difference from our conceptions of them, and their independent importance.

On this picture, to repeat, the background transcends the individual not by endowing her with value or exceeding her in value, but by exceeding what she can fully comprehend at any given time while properly stirring the desire to learn more about what she does not fully comprehend. What comprises the background is not a deity, nor a social or historical process, nor a tradition, but other socially situated human individuals, conceived as unique, not fully surveyable, and in need of love to be understood—individuals who are themselves confronted by the same vast, intricate and exacting manifold. This, we could say, is Murdoch's sketch of the "here" where we all are, a "here" which racism and other modern tribalisms seek to repudiate.

There is room in this picture for concepts such as "submission," "obedience," and (yes) "sovereignty," but not as tools, descriptors, or props of *social* hierarchy. There is nothing here to suggest that individuals should submit to traditional forms of authority or that they derive their value from the background. In particular, the agent is called upon not to obey or to command other individuals but to "make discoveries" about them, to learn about them and to appreciate their separateness and difference from herself and from others. The agent is given to understand, moreover, that such gains in understanding will only be possible through an exercise of love. This is a naturalistic picture that has been deftly modified to capture what Murdoch took to be the regulative principle of liberalism, the idea that human beings are "substantial, impenetrable, individual, indefinable, and valuable" (AD: 294).

On the reading presented here, Murdoch's modified naturalistic picture of the individual is not meant to replace the liberal outlook's romantic picture of the individual (as one who heroically imparts value to a valueless world through her choices). It is meant to condition and complement it, so that liberal societies are better equipped, at a conceptual level, to realize their ideals. The basic idea is simple: to conceive of others as unique, never fully within one's grasp, and revealed in essential ways through love is to encourage a perpetual modesty about one's understandings of them together with a modicum of curiosity. Such modesty and curiosity, in turn, prime us to experience the separateness of other persons, their importance, and their right to live in a way that makes sense to them even when it doesn't make sense to us (or to others). In Murdoch's more evocative terms: conceiving of others as unique, transcendent, and revealed by love primes us to experience their reality even, or especially, when we are prone to losing sight of it.

2.11 Summary

In this section I've sketched what Murdoch calls the liberal and naturalistic outlooks, considered how well each one supports the liberal sensibility or spirit that liberal democracies depend upon, and examined how Murdoch articulates a modified version of the naturalistic outlook to better support the liberal sensibility. At the heart of Murdoch's analysis is the idea that the modern world needs to recover the premodern idea of a reality that transcends the individual if it is to realize its own ideal of a society in which individuals live together as free equals. On Murdoch's modified version of the naturalistic outlook, human individuals conceived as unique, transcendent, and revealed by love constitute just such a reality. Although these three features of the individual coalesce in Murdoch's account, it is useful to consider them separately.[61] Accordingly, in Section 3 I examine the uniqueness and transcendence of individuals, while in Section 4 I examine their knowability through love. Taken together, in these two sections I show how Murdoch understands, anchors, and interconnects these features, and I consider more closely their connection to the liberal sensibility that Murdoch cherishes.

3 The Unique and Transcendent Individual

The possibilities that exist between two people, or among a group of people, are a kind of alchemy. They are the most interesting thing in life.[62]

3.1 Introduction

In Section 2 I compared what Murdoch calls the liberal and naturalistic outlooks and showed how Murdoch develops a nonhierarchical version of the naturalistic outlook to frame her conception of the individual and to better serve Enlightenment ideals. On Murdoch's articulation of the naturalistic outlook, the individual is seen against a background that *transcends* him but does not eclipse or *subordinate* him; it thus preserves the individual's unconditional value. The background itself consists in other individuals conceived as unique, transcendent, and knowable through love. In this section I examine the first two of these features of Murdoch's naturalized individual.

---

[61] Two qualifications are in order. First, these are the central features of Murdoch's conception of the individual, not the only features. Second, Murdoch uses a range of modifiers to convey the ideas that individuals are unique and that they transcend one another's understanding (e.g., impenetrable, form-defying, indefinable, not fully definable, boundless, opaque, endlessly particular, endlessly to be explained, infinitely particular). Some of these modifiers contain other ideas as well.

[62] Rich 1979: 193.

It will be helpful to begin with an example, or foil, from Kazuo Ishiguro's *Klara and the Sun* (2021).

Klara is the android friend of Josie, a young woman with a serious illness caused by the same creepy "lifting" procedure that earlier led to her older sister's death. The novel asks whether, with enough mapping and programming, Klara can be turned into – literally "continue" – Josie, should Josie die. Or is there, as the character Mr. Capaldi puts it, "something unreachable inside each of us. Something that's unique and won't transfer"? Mr. Capaldi himself considers this a quaint idea, a piece of reactionary nostalgia. "There's nothing there," he assures Josie's mom, "nothing inside Josie that's beyond the Klaras of this world to continue" (2021: 207–208). Josie's mom, of course, both does and does not want to believe him.

Murdoch's conception of the individual affirms, precisely, that there is "something unreachable" and "unique" in each person. This way of thinking about persons is continuous with what Murdoch takes to be the core tenet of liberal democracy – the idea that persons are "substantial, impenetrable, individual, indefinable, and valuable" (AD: 294). What Murdoch offers us, then, is *a way of understanding ourselves* that she takes to be at the heart of Enlightenment values. The idea that individuals are unique and transcendent (and revealed by love) is not, for Murdoch, a matter of empirical fact; it is a *regulative ideal*. It is an idea "that we need and use" (TL: 38).[63] It captures a way of seeing ourselves that Murdoch takes to be ordinary, valuable, coherent, and at risk of being lost.

What exactly is at stake in how we see ourselves? A great deal, Murdoch believes. We conceptualize ourselves, she says, "at a point of great conceptual sensibility" (ME: 75). That is, how we picture ourselves has real consequences for what we become, for what we are (and so for everything else in the world). "Man is a creature who makes pictures of himself and then comes to resemble the picture" (ME: 75). A world in which we saw ourselves and one another as Mr. Capaldi sees Josie would, Murdoch implies, be a world in which Capaldi's reductive picture of us was closer to the truth, just as a world in which we saw one another as machines would be a world in which we were indeed more machine-like. This, for Murdoch, is part of the immense importance of philosophy and the arts.

Murdoch doesn't try to *prove* that humans in fact possess the features of uniqueness, transcendence, or knowability by love – features Mr. Capaldi rejects. Regulative ideals cannot be proven: they are the kind of idea "about

---

[63] Here, and in the paragraph after the next (where I also cite TL), I'm quoting Murdoch's comments about the regulative status of the idea that thoughts are inner experiences and extending them to the idea of the individual, which she calls "an ideal of reason" (IP: 41).

which it makes no sense to ask, is it true or false that it is *so*" (TL: 39). We can, however, see her as doing something more subtle. With a bit of reconstruction, we can see the essays in *Sovereignty* (in particular) as filling in and grounding these features by showing how each one is connected to other ideas that are familiar, important, and plausible.[64] Establishing these features is not Murdoch's principal aim in these essays (or elsewhere), so reading her in this way does require reconstruction. But the materials are plainly there, and they bring out both a conceptual coherence and a political significance to Murdoch's early and middle writings that might otherwise escape one. Murdoch doesn't suggest that we *always* do (or should) think of others in the light of this regulative ideal. Her suggestion is rather that envisaging others in this way has an important place in ordinary life for good reason, and that members of democratic societies have particular reason to want it to continue to have such a place.

3.2 Uniqueness

Let's begin by considering the idea of individuals as unique. We (seem to) apprehend the uniqueness of others in their faces, their voices, their body language, and countless other ways, and we take it to have depth, to reach into their thoughts and experience. We assume that identical twins who were raised together, for all their physical similarities, are different "inside." When someone whom we love dies, we feel that a distinctive inner world dies along with them; this is part of what we grieve. Our sense that others are unique, and substantially so, helps explain why we're both fascinated by and disturbed at the prospect of Klara "continuing" Josie. (Is it possible to replicate a being who is truly unique? What would this mean exactly?)

For Murdoch, the uniqueness of individuals is an important idea in its own right and something that helps to illuminate the differences between people. Uniqueness implies that differences between people are inevitable – a primitive fact, if you like – and that they run deep. Murdoch considers it a serious failing of the liberal outlook examined in Section 2 that it cannot do justice either to the uniqueness of individuals, as we commonly think of it, or to the gravity and extent of the differences among them. On Murdoch's analysis, as we saw, the liberal individual is not much of an individual at all. The individuality of a person is confined to his will, understood as his explicit choices or outward actions (IP: 21). This leaves nothing for differences between individuals to be about, Murdoch observes, except differences of choice, and, more precisely,

---

[64] "[A] theory ... is the more attractive the more it explains, the more its structure may be seen as underlying things which are familiar to us in ordinary life" (IP: 33). At the same time (and citing Wittgenstein), Murdoch rejects the idea that being "irresistibly inclined" to say something makes it true (IP: 16).

differences of choice where the facts are settled (as when we agree that the neighbor's dog is barking at all hours but disagree about what to do about it.) For Murdoch, many cases of disagreement are nothing like this. Often, we disagree about how to construe the facts, how to describe a situation. We don't just make different choices in such cases, she says, "we see different worlds" (VC: 41/82). That this is so, that we see the world differently from one another, is at the heart of the *human* sublime to which Murdoch appeals in SBR and S&G. What properly stuns us, she says there, "is not, as Kant imagined, the formlessness of nature, but rather its unutterable particularity; and most particular and individual of all natural things is the mind of man" (S&G: 215).[65]

3.3 Uniqueness and Democracy

Before examining Murdoch's elucidation of the idea that individuals are unique, I want to consider first the potential political significance of her emphasis on particularity and difference. One worry we might have is that stressing the differences between people is often *the problem* where toleration and related attitudes are concerned. There is an arresting moment in the "Eyes on the Prize" documentary series about the U.S. civil rights movement when a white reporter speaks to a young white girl (perhaps ten years old) about the violent resistance of some whites to the admission of Black students into her school (Vecchione 1987). By way of explanation, the girl remarks that (American) Blacks are "more different to us" than other kinds of people such as "Chinese or Spanish." (It's unclear if she is referring to Chinese- or Spanish- *Americans*.) But what's being asserted here is precisely *not* the uniqueness of individual Blacks (or whites). Instead, the girl sees Black and white Americans as having immutable characteristics corresponding to their racial group. That is, she asserts what Appiah calls "racialism" (1990: 4–5). She has been taught, moreover, that these characteristics make it inappropriate for Black and white children to share public space. This follows a familiar pattern for the creation of de facto social hierarchies. Members of one social group (e.g., Christian, male, white, European) are taken to be essentially the same as one another, and in a way that distinguishes them permanently from members of a competing social group (e.g., Muslim, female, Black, African). The alleged differences are then used to justify the domination or annihilation of the one group by the other (see, e.g., Fredrickson 2002: ch. 3). Murdoch's emphasis on the uniqueness of individuals works against this. To see *individuals* as different from one another is to see

---

[65] Murdoch adds: "That is incidentally why tragedy is the highest art, because it is most intensely concerned with the most individual thing" (S&G: 215). Other places where Murdoch implicitly or explicitly affirms the uniqueness of individuals include: SRR:148; S&G: 219; SBR: 270/284; MDH: 38.

them as not reducible to any social identity. In that case, the fact that a person is male or British or Jewish or nonbinary or wealthy will not exhaust who the person is (though such facts may be critically important in many contexts).[66] Something essential will be left over, something that is the individual's alone, and that distinguishes him from other individuals whose social identities are identical to his own.

A subtler point: one who sees individuals as unique will expect to find a diversity of views within any social group, no matter how small or seemingly homogeneous. Such a person will trust that vegans (for instance) will not think exactly alike, any more than all Baptist Christians will. And this means that such a person will recognize the potential for disagreement among members within any one social group and, therewith, the potential for the formation of unprecedented political alliances between groups or their individual members. Such a person will recognize, that is, that *some* Baptist Christians may be receptive to animal welfare (and vice-versa). The potential for such new alliances is crucial to democracy because it ensures that there is no permanent majority, that is, no ruling class. *Belief* in this potential is also crucial to democracy because it gives people of divergent interests or camps a reason to talk and listen to each other, and a reason to think that their ends can be democratically advanced. Murdoch's emphasis on the uniqueness of individuals underlines this potential.

3.4 Uniqueness and Historicity

Murdoch relates the uniqueness of individuals to their *historicity*. "[W]e are," she says, "human historical individuals" (IP: 28). We can distinguish in Murdoch two senses in which human individuals are historical. First, humans are for Murdoch historical in the general sense that our lives unfold within a specific socio-historical moment, amid determinate material conditions, where the concepts at our disposal are conditioned by this moment and these conditions (VC: 43/84). That is, I will have a different concept of loyalty, or of gender, or of self, than I would were I living in the fourteenth century, and I will lack entirely some concepts that a version of me who witnessed the Black Death would possess (and vice-versa). This is to say that for Murdoch there is no "absolute" perspective for an individual or culture to occupy. Murdoch, however, is not a relativist. She embraces the possibility of moral objectivity; she simply doesn't tie that objectivity in any way to a timeless perspective. Nor is she a determinist. She stresses that we're able to reject or to revise the concepts

---

[66] Nothing in Murdoch's picture implies that we should *ignore* a person's social identity as, for instance, theories of racial colorblindness recommend.

we inherit, as well as to generate new ones; this, for Murdoch, is an important sense in which humans are free (ME: 71–72; OGG: 73).

Second, humans are for Murdoch historical in the sense that each of us has a *personal* history that distinguishes us from other individuals. This personal sense of the historical is important for our purposes because Murdoch takes it to be the case that one's personal history gives a unique shape, or inflection, to the concepts one uses (IP: 25–33). We could illustrate this by saying that when my friend describes someone as "serious" I know what she means, but my use of this concept is somewhat different – my *conception* of what it means to be "serious" differs from hers – because my use of this concept has grown out of different life experiences. This is true even though my friend and I share a great deal in the way of culture and social identity and history. (We did *not*, e.g., share a family, or a hometown, nor did we share innumerable experiences.) She and I share most concepts, in other words, but these concepts have ramified somewhat differently in our two individual cases. The two senses of history to which Murdoch appeals are obviously related: we are born into certain sets of concepts, based on our socio-historical location; those concepts then undergo continual revision and ramification, based on our personal experience and in response to changes in the wider culture.

For Murdoch, then, every (adult) individual has a distinctive ramification, or network, of concepts tied to their life history, and this network is at the heart of that person's sense of the world. In Murdoch's terms, it determines their "total vision of life," meaning their distinctive modus operandi, expressed in such things as "their mode of speech or silence, their choice of words, ... what they think attractive or praiseworthy, what they find funny: in short the configurations of their thought which show continually in their reactions and conversation" (VC: 39/80–81). Murdoch also uses the metaphor of texture – "texture of a man's being" – to describe what is at issue here. In insisting on the uniqueness of a person's mindedness or mode of being, Murdoch is not denying that people may be highly conformist in their thinking, or suggesting that we are free to assign any meaning we like to words or concepts.[67] She is saying, rather, that an individual's way of seeing and experiencing things, like a person's spoken or written language, possesses distinguishing features, even as it conforms to more general patterns.[68]

---

[67] Wiseman 2020 distinguishes Murdoch's position from the idea (attacked by Wittgenstein) of a private language.

[68] The distinctiveness of an individual's use of language has notable forensic value; it was the Unabomber's "linguistic fingerprint" that led to his detection (Kreuz 2023).

3.5 Transcendence

The idea that individuals transcend one another's understanding, that they are in some sense "unreachable," is, perhaps, less routine than the idea that individuals are unique. Let's consider what Murdoch makes of it.

The idea is not simply that individuals are not fully comprehensible to one another. This would not be saying much: no one expects perfect knowledge of others and few would wish to be perfectly understood by others (John 2013). The idea is rather that others elude our understanding in important ways. The story of Josie and Klara is again helpful in bringing out what is at stake.

Josie's father (Mr. P) and Klara discuss Klara's assignment to "continue" Josie, should Josie – like her sister – die prematurely. Mr. P asks:

> Do you believe in the human heart? I don't mean simply the organ, obviously. I'm speaking in the poetic sense. The human heart. Do you think there is such a thing? Something that makes each of us special and individual? And if we just suppose that there is. Then don't you think, in order to truly learn Josie, you'd have to learn not just her mannerisms but what's deeply inside her? Wouldn't you have to learn her heart? ... And that could be difficult, no? Something beyond even your wonderful capabilities. Because an impersonation wouldn't do, however skillful. You'd have to learn her heart, and learn it fully, or you'll never become Josie in any sense that matters (Ishiguro 2021: 215–216).

After reflecting for a moment, Klara replies: "Of course, a human heart is bound to be complex. But it must be limited. Even if Mr. P is talking in the poetic sense, there'll be an end to what there is to learn." For Murdoch, to say that individuals transcend one another's understanding is to say – by contrast – that that there will *never* be "an end to what there is to learn" about others, to what it would be *good* to learn about others. So even if one were somehow able to capture a person's life experiences – their distinctive history – in its entirety (as Mr. Capaldi seeks to do with respect to Josie), that person would still elude one in important ways. Murdoch effectively develops and grounds this idea of transcendence in three different ways: historically, existentially, and psychologically.

Let's begin with the role of history in grounding the idea that we transcend one another's understanding.

By any account, to live inside of history means not only that one's concepts will bear the imprint of one's past but that one's concepts are subject to alteration in both the present and the future. My friend will have new experiences that bear on her sense of what it means for someone to be "serious." Murdoch takes it that concepts ramify and interconnect: "It is especially characteristic of normative words ... to belong to sets or patterns without an appreciation of which they cannot be understood" (IP: 32). Changes in one concept therefore betoken changes in others; as my friend comes to think differently about seriousness, she'll also begin to think differently about other things (e.g., frivolity, small talk, tact). "[A]s we move and as we look our concepts are themselves changing" (IP: 25). To be a "human historical individual" is thus to be subject to perpetual alteration, to be in formation (and not necessarily for the better, in Murdoch's view). Now it is impossible to comprehend once and for all a being whose development is ongoing, particularly when that development may be affected by our interactions with it (including very much the effort to comprehend the being in question). This is doubly true when those who seek to do the comprehending are themselves subject to history, and so to alteration, on an ongoing basis. These basic observations about what it is to be a "human historical individual" indicate one sense that Murdoch gives to the idea that individuals transcend our understanding.

A second, "existential" sense Murdoch gives to the notion that individuals transcend one another turns on the idea that *ordinary reality* itself is elusive, that it exceeds what we can compass. In characterizing the elusiveness of reality, Murdoch appeals to the idea that there is no pattern or figure outside of human life, such as God or the stages of History, that can make sense of everything that happens within it (OGG: 69–72; SGC, 77, 96–98). Unrepentant Nazis live out their final years comfortably in Argentina. A chance meeting changes the course of one's life. There is, in short, an irreducible element of contingency, or randomness, to how things play out. Murdoch also ties the elusiveness of reality to the sheer magnitude, variety, and complexity of the world. It is teeming with concepts, wars, viruses, cultures, works of art, other species, volcanoes, and on and on, as well as possessing other persons in countless and evolving relations with one another. We can, of course, discern patterns in all of this. Murdoch's point is that the patterns don't exhaust the phenomena. The closest we can get to a master pattern, in Murdoch's view, is the good. This provides a "shadowy" kind of order, an intimation of order, that leaves much to be explained and suffered (SGC: 77). From this perspective, we can't definitively survey others, in part, because we can't quite compass the situations and the larger world in which their lives unfold; we can't nail down the big picture.

Although the idea that reality outstrips our understanding is hardly unfamiliar, it *is* contentious in a way that the notion that we live in time is not. Not everyone thinks of the world as "aimless, chancy, and huge" (SGC: 97). There are countless forms of the belief that everything falls into place when seen in the proper light. (A nineteen-year-old Murdoch seems to me to express a communist version of such a belief in a letter to a friend: "I feel now that I am doing *some* good, and that life has a purpose and that the history of civilisation is not just an interesting series of unconnected muddles, but a comprehensible development towards the highest stage of society, the Soviet world state" (Horner and Rowe 2016: 10).) So this is a juncture where it's important to keep in mind that Murdoch is not trying to prove to sceptics that individuals transcend our understanding. It is more accurate to see her as working to elucidate and secure this tenet for those who have already made it a part of their lives, yet may – like Josie's parents – feel pressure to relinquish it. Murdoch seeks to show that it is not rationally compulsory to abandon this way of seeing others.[69] In this vein, she notes that works of tragedy leave the reader (or spectator) in intense doubt and that, curiously, this seems to be a part of their revelatory force (S&G: esp. 219). We can never be sure why Othello trusted Iago as he did or what drove Iago to such sadistic extremes, but we do remember these characters and our inability to fully fathom them or their destinies. Murdoch says, in effect, isn't this real life? To think so is certainly no more contentious (or unusual) than believing that everything and everyone falls into place when seen in the proper light. What is more, Murdoch takes there to be something morally questionable about such certainty. She connects it, as we will see in the final part of this section, to escapism.[70]

The picture so far is that human individuals encounter one another in the midst of a larger and constantly unfolding scene, a scene that they do not view in the same way, neither exactly nor sometimes at all, and which is never thoroughly comprehensible to them. They are not only different from each other in significant ways. They are different from – more than – whatever conceptions other individuals may hold of them. No one's conception of another *fully maps* that other, as Mr. Capaldi intends to map Josie. Nor are any two conceptions of a given individual incomplete in exactly the same way. In Murdoch's words: "We have only a segment of the circle" (S&G: 216). Murdoch connects these aspects of our situation to two familiar and credible ideas: that we live inside history and that we're not able fully to understand or explain the nature of our existence.

Let us now consider the third, psychological sense that Murdoch gives to the idea that individuals transcend our understanding. At this point, we encounter one of the most important additions that *Sovereignty* makes to Murdoch's overall account: the idea of the psyche. Inspired by Freud, the psyche designates

---

[69] Just as Murdoch argues, in ME and VC, that even though it is impossible to *demonstrate* the existence of transcendent entities, it does not follow that *belief* in them is irrational.

[70] Murdoch notes that religion may, but need not, be a form of escapism (e.g., SGC: 98–99). But where religion is not escapist, the believer has the problem of how to reconcile evil and suffering with God's plan. In the end, for Murdoch, both the believer and the non-believer face the difficulty "of looking properly at evil and human suffering" (OGG: 71).

for Murdoch a powerful "energy system" or "mechanism" that influences one in ways that (often) escape one's awareness and that are resolutely egocentric in nature (SGC: 81; OGG: 50).[71] "[M]ost of what is often called 'will' or 'willing' belongs to this system" (OGG: 65). Because the psyche is egocentric, and because it works in stealth, it severely threatens one's ability to reach a clear perception of others, to appreciate their reality.

There are different ways to understand Murdoch's claim that the psyche is egocentric. One can take her to be saying that we're all *arrogant*, that we suffer from delusions of superiority or grandeur (e.g., OGG: 57). I think Murdoch is more convincing, however, when she connects egocentricity to hedonism and, specifically, to the attempt to avoid the pain that comes from *facing reality* and the corresponding attraction to perspectives that offer more comfort (OGG: 62). Facing reality is bound to be painful (as well as exhilarating) on Murdoch's picture. It presents us, as we have seen, with mind-blowing magnitude and complexity, as well as with immense suffering. Human beings are both limited in their ability to comprehend or command reality and intimately implicated in the suffering it contains. Reality also confronts us with the atomic smallness of our lives in the grand scheme of things. But what does this have to do with egocentricity? Murdoch suggests that the psyche deals with this state of affairs by casting its possessor as the subjective center of the world, thereby investing him with inordinate significance or power. This needn't take the form of believing oneself to be superior to others; it could just as well take the form of an inferiority complex or paranoia.[72] At its most dangerous, the psyche generates self-centric "fantasy" versions of other people and events that one mistakes for reality and that thereby insulate one from reality. One's perceived greatness or inadequacy, one's personal experience or history and one's fears or desires take center stage and everything else falls into shadow, seems less real.[73] Such fantasies are, Murdoch thinks, part of our natural psychology, something with which we must contend in ourselves and in others (SGC: 77, 82). They form part of the "here" where we all are.

In addition to being egocentric, the psyche is "highly individual and personal" (OGG: 53).[74] I take Murdoch to mean by this that the psyche exploits the

---

[71] Murdoch also uses the terms "ego" and "self" to refer to the psyche (OGG, 51; SGC, 98). Murdoch's discussion of the psyche is found in OGG: 50–53 and SGC: 76–77.

[72] As Manguso notes: "Preferable to accepting one's insignificance is imagining the others hate you" (2017: 37). Perhaps the closest Murdoch comes to discussing this type of possibility is in her discussion of masochism: "[T]he ideas of guilt and punishment can be the most subtle tool of the ingenious self" (OGG: 66; SGC: 85, 97).

[73] Simone Weil: "[B]eing seems to us less and less concentrated the farther it is removed from us" (1978 [1951]: 99).

[74] In one place Murdoch describes the psyche *itself* as an individual, "a historically determined individual relentlessly looking after itself" (SGC: 76). For Murdoch, human individuals are historically conditioned but, as noted in 3.4, not *determined*.

individual's personal history and infiltrates her outlook to pursue its ends. That is to say: individuals will have their own (evolving) ways of not facing up to reality, of centering themselves at the expense of others, their own specific imagery or chain of associations that resonate for them. This does not rule out the possibility that the psyche may work through collective systems of thought or imagery, but it implies that these systems must find a home in the agent (Panizza 2022: 70). In effect, Murdoch offers an account of why it is that we are often willing to accept remarkably pernicious and crude forms of conventional thinking: because to do so shields us from aspects of reality that we may find hard to bear. This is to think of such phenomena as racism or antisemitism or misogyny – instances of "convention" – as collective channels of reality-avoidance. Admittedly, these pathologies may play out very differently in members of dominant groups than in those who are dominated. In particular, they often lead members of subordinate groups to center *others* at their own expense. Murdoch's account of the psyche does not seem made for such cases, but it does suggest an interesting approach to them. It is an approach, moreover, that allows us to recognize structural forces as part of the problem (insofar as those forces facilitate reality-avoidance). We can then see "neurosis" as a more purely idiosyncratic channel for reality-avoidance and treat these two channels as powerfully reinforcing one another, with conventional tropes feeding into personal obsessions and vice-versa, much as Murdoch suggests (SBR: 254/268).

The addition of the psyche to the picture means that not only will individuals necessarily have *incomplete* or partial conceptions of each other, they will often have *distorted* conceptions of one another. Misconceptions. Particularly in the right (or wrong!) conditions, such as when people feel frightened or disoriented, or when their access to information has been compromised. The existence of the psyche implies that we will not merely fail to see everything worth seeing about others. We will, in addition, sometimes see things that aren't there to be seen, or distort them beyond recognition in spite of ourselves.[75] This is the psychological sense in which, for Murdoch, individuals are transcendent to one another. It means that even if others weren't unique and ongoing parts of a reality we cannot fully fathom, we still wouldn't (normally) succeed in comprehending them – far from it. Murdoch grounds this darker sense of transcendence, as she does the historical and existential senses, in commonplace ideas – in this case, the notions that reality is often painful to face and that egocentricity helps us to avoid actually facing reality in ways that often escape our awareness.

---

[75] As, it seems, Murdoch's hero Kant did when he mistook the richly justified distress of young Maria von Herbert for female hysteria (Langton 1992).

3.6 Summary

Taking stock. We've been considering the transcendent background to the individual on Murdoch's modified version of the naturalistic outlook. In Section 2 we noted that this background consists in other individuals and their relations with each other, conceived as unique, transcendent, and knowable through love. In this section we examined the first two of these features. We noted that Murdoch connects them to the historicity of persons, the elusiveness of the larger scene within which we encounter one another, and the difficulty, for human beings, of facing reality. For all of these reasons, Murdoch suggests, individuals properly present themselves to one another as unreachable, as beings who are not amenable to Mr. Capaldi's ambitions. Unique and transcendent.

This way of thinking about individuals precludes reductive conceptions of them. It implies that each person is a unique world and that any representation of a person that we form (or encounter) can capture at most a fragment of the whole. It thus encourages a kind of agnosticism and curiosity that, as we noted in Section 2, Murdoch associates with toleration (2.7). This is presumably why the attributes of uniqueness and transcendence figure (in so many words) in Murdoch's description of liberalism's prime article of faith: the belief that persons are "substantial, impenetrable, individual, indefinable, and valuable" (AD: 294).

What we have not yet addressed is the third feature of Murdoch's concept of the individual: the idea that the individual is revealed by love. To this we turn in the next section. We should note that *this* idea does not appear in Murdoch's description of liberalism's prime tenet. What is more, love might seem out of place where politics is concerned. But, as we will see, Murdoch takes the idea that the individual is revealed by love to be naturally connected to the ideas that individuals are transcendent and unique, and just as ordinary as these ideas. In this way, Murdoch obliges us to consider the possibility that love, too, belongs with a liberal sensibility.

4 The Individual Revealed by Love

> *It was an idea so simple that Bassam wondered how he had ignored it for so long: they too had families, histories, shadows.*[76]

4.1 Introduction

In Section 2 I compared the liberal and naturalistic outlooks and showed how Murdoch articulates a nonhierarchical version of the naturalistic outlook to support her concept of the individual and to better serve the liberal ideals she

---
[76] McCann 2020: 28.

cherishes. In Section 3 I examined the first two features of that concept: the uniqueness and transcendence of the individual. In this section, and to complete my analysis, I examine the third feature of Murdoch's concept of the individual: his dependence on love for a knowledge of other individuals. This feature is *epistemological*: it concerns how we come to know other individuals and what it means to know them.

For Murdoch, any serious view of morality must recognize and elucidate the importance of love. One of Murdoch's sharpest criticisms of the moral philosophy of her day – scholarship that she sees as unconsciously embodying the liberal outlook – is that it fails to find a place for love in the moral life (e.g., IP: 2; OGG: 45). Murdoch herself, by contrast, places love at the very center of her ethics.

Let me put this in perspective. In 2.2 I represented the liberal and naturalistic outlooks in terms of four postulates. It will be helpful here to compare their different versions of the third postulate, starting with the liberal outlook.

> (3L) Freedom consists in choosing for oneself how to connect facts to values; the facts are wholly available to any rational observer and motivationally inert.

According to the naturalistic outlook, and in contrast:

> (3N) Freedom originates in knowledge of self and world; such knowledge is necessarily partial and possesses practical force.

Murdoch's reworking of naturalism in effect tells us that the knowledge in question – the knowledge indicated in 3N – comes through (or consists in) *love* and that its prime object is reality in the form of other socially-situated human individuals. "Love is the perception of individuals. Love is the extremely difficult realization that something other than oneself is real. Love ... is the discovery of reality" (S&G: 215). Murdoch speaks of love equally as the knowledge of individuals and as the activity, quality, or disposition that seeks such knowledge.

There are naturally many ways to approach the concept of love in Murdoch's writings and much has been written about it.[77] We should note, too, that Murdoch recognizes more than one kind of human love. For these reasons and others, my discussion in this section will be highly selective. I will focus on the idea of love as *knowledge*, love as giving us a knowledge of reality that nothing else does. I'll examine Murdoch's development of this idea in her early and middle writings by tracing love's relation to freedom, compassion, and attention.[78]

---

[77] I will cite some of the relevant scholarship as I go.

[78] Murdoch's later writings speak more of *eros* and may introduce new considerations.

4.2 Freedom

For Murdoch, the serious exploration of reality – particularly when that reality is (or concerns) other persons – often involves the exercise of imagination, the conjuring of possibilities "which go beyond what could be said to be strictly factual" (DPR: 198). In our efforts to understand other persons and events we imagine, as best we can, what it would be like, say, to lose your job, or to discover that you were adopted, or to fly to the moon. Love, as Murdoch conceives it, plays an important part in such truth-directed exercises of imagination. This makes love a site of freedom.

Murdoch connects love to at least two kinds of freedom. First, and most straightforwardly, love frees us *from* powerful reality-avoidant forms of thinking (convention, neurosis, fantasy) and it frees us *to* explore what confronts us in creative and fruitful ways.[79] Love frees us to investigate what we see, or think we see, in ways that are neither prefabricated nor simply a matter of fact-checking. This positive freedom is, for Murdoch, the flip side of freedom *from* the straitjackets of convention, neurosis, and fantasy. Let us call this "primary freedom."

Importantly, on Murdoch's telling, even as love frees us to investigate others in rich and fruitful ways – *because* it frees us to do this – it also confronts us with the otherness and difference of other persons. And in confronting this primitive fact, Murdoch suggests, we experience (or become aware of) a second and darker kind of freedom, what she calls "tragic freedom." In her words:

> The tragic freedom implied by love is this: that we all have an indefinitely extended capacity to imagine the being of others. Tragic, because there is no prefabricated harmony, and others are, to an extent we never cease discovering, different from ourselves. Nor is there any social totality within which we can come to comprehend differences as placed and reconciled. We have only a segment of the circle. Freedom is exercised in the confrontation by each other, in the context of an infinitely extensible work of imaginative understanding, of two irreducibly dissimilar individuals. Love is the imaginative recognition of, that is respect for, this otherness (S&G: 216).

Let me highlight some of the main points in this rather challenging passage. Murdoch tells us that love is the *imaginative* recognition of, respect for, the ways that others are different and separate from ourselves and from each other. That is, love is a recognition of difference and "otherness" arrived at, in part, through imagination. Through this exercise of love we are liberated from more limited ways of thinking, we enjoy what I called above our primary freedom. This loving recognition of difference, in turn, *implies* something further, namely that we have "an indefinitely extended capacity to imagine the being of others."

---

[79] Love's "enemies," Murdoch tells us, are convention and fantasy (S&G: 216; SBR: 254/268).

Why think *that*? Our capacity to imagine the being of others is indefinitely extended, Murdoch says, because others are different in ways "we never cease discovering." That is – and contrary to what Mr. Capaldi and Klara suppose – we never finish learning the ways that others differ from ourselves or from our conceptions of them (3.5). Because we never finish learning these differences – to continue Murdoch's thought – we can be said to have an unlimited capacity to imagine (and reimagine) the being of others. In exercising this capacity, we express a second kind of freedom, a freedom that Murdoch describes as tragic in character.

These ideas raise many questions. For our purposes, I consider two of them. First, why consider such freedom *tragic*? Murdoch tells us that the freedom that love implies is tragic because what we discover through love is, first, that individuals are truly different from one another and, second, that there is no "social totality within which we can come to comprehend" or reconcile these differences. We can think of such a totality as a systematic whole, such as the socio-cosmological order that shaped and ordered the lives of Keaja and Tselane. Murdoch compares such a totality to a *circle*. "We have only a segment of the circle" – meaning, I think, that we cannot grasp the whole that would make perfect sense of the individual parts (in this case, human individuals and their relations to one another). We cannot grasp the whole because what we discover through love is, as Justin Broackes puts it, "the boundless variety of free persons."[80] In other words, there *is* no systematic whole, or at least none that we can grasp. There is only a plurality of free persons, endlessly different from one another, in relationships that are also endlessly different from one another. Unique and transcendent.

Still, why should Murdoch (or we) consider this state of affairs to be tragic? Why should the boundless variety of free persons not be a source of delight or relief (or indifference)? It can seem positively *illiberal* to suppose that it must be grievous or distressing, and in our earlier discussion of the idea of uniqueness, we touched on one of the reasons why: democracy depends on citizens believing that the will of the majority can shift, that new kinds of alliances and relationships between people are always possible (3.3). Murdoch certainly recognizes that difference or diversity can be a deep source of pleasure (e.g., SBR: 269/ 283). But here she is registering that it also contains the potential for enduring conflict, misunderstanding, frustration, and fear. Real diversity means that harmony is not prefabricated or assured: it is something that must be achieved and that is precarious. This is particularly so when there is no given way to

---

[80] Broackes 2012: 32. I have found Broackes' entire (and brief) discussion of S&G and SBR helpful (32–34).

harmonize the different ends that individuals hold, no "social totality" within which to comprehend them. We might contrast this with a social hierarchy of the sort we discussed in 2.3. In a hierarchical society, differences *can* be "placed and reconciled": everyone has her part to play in an interrelated whole and (when things go as they are supposed to) people find purpose and contentment in fulfilling their respective roles. One has determinate universal standards with which to make sense of serious differences (e.g., in ways of life, religious convictions, sexual orientation, or political ideals) and with which to hold others to account. Here, in contrast – where we take individuals to be endlessly various and free – we must continually *find* common purpose or ground, however temporary, and we must do it from positions that are limited: "[w]e have only a segment of the circle." We cannot appeal to a socio-cosmological order, or some other form of systematic whole, to reconcile our differences nor to make sense of them. We have no guarantee, in the end, that they make any sense.

Those who aspire to a liberal sensibility may rightly celebrate diversity, then, but if we take that diversity to be radical – as Murdoch does – we may also find it, at times, to be disquieting. For one thing, it means that there is no guarantee that *others* will delight in diversity, or that we can reach a clear understanding of why this is so in any given case. We may find this tragic.

A second question is: why connect any of this with *love*? Why not *simply* speak of "tolerance" or "open-mindedness" or "respect"?[81] Murdoch has clearly drawn inspiration here from Simone Weil, who connected love to a recognition of the existence of others.[82] Still: why should we speak this way? Why associate love with knowledge at all? It's true that people are more willing to confide in, or "be themselves" around, those they feel loved by. Murdoch is certainly registering this point, but she's saying much more. She holds that even in contexts where the willingness to let down one's guard is not relevant, a loving regard is capable of revealing deeply significant aspects of others, and of the world, that might otherwise escape one. She rejects the identification of "what is real" or "what is objectively true" with "what a clinical perspective discloses," no matter how acute or sophisticated that perspective might be. She maintains that, as Broackes puts it, "[i]nstead of allowing into reality only what meets a 'scientific' requirement ... we should

---

[81] Murdoch plays with this idea in SBR. After identifying the readiness to view others as possessing "a right to exist and to have a separate mode of being which is important and interesting to themselves" with tolerance or "Liberal spirit," she adds "we may decide later that 'tolerance' is too mild a word for this capacity at its highest." Murdoch thinks that the better name for this is "love" (SBR: 257, 269–271/284–285). Elsewhere in the essay Murdoch speaks of a "loving toleration" (SBR: 263/277).

[82] "Among human beings, only the existence of those we love is fully recognized." "Belief in the existence of other human beings as such is *love*" (Weil 2002 [1952]: 64).

allow the world to contain all that meets the gaze of a just and loving moral perceiver" (2012: 46–47).

Here again the postulates introduced in 2.2 may be helpful. Recall postulates 2L and 2N.

(2L) Fact and value are entirely separate; value is a product of the will, not a genuine part of the world.

(2N) Fact and value are interlinked; value is a genuine part of the world or universe.

When Murdoch links love to knowledge, she in effect rejects 2L in favor of 2N, and she shows us *how* she construes 2N, that is, how she links fact to value. Namely, by holding that certain facts are only available, or accessible, from within a loving (and so evaluative) perspective. In keeping with postulate 3N (which equates freedom with knowledge, rather than choice), Murdoch maintains that the knowledge so acquired is both freeing and partial. It frees us from limited ways of thinking about others and thereby makes us aware of our unlimited capacity to imagine their being.

4.3 Compassion

Murdoch's commitment to the epistemological importance of love was, and to some extent remains, philosophically unorthodox.[83] Murdoch embraces this controversial position because she believes that, given the kind of creatures we are, opening ourselves to reality is an operation in which *compassion* plays a decisive role.[84] This is partly why, for Murdoch, knowledge of reality is a *moral* achievement and aspiration, as much as it is an intellectual one.

The root meaning of the (Latinate) term "compassion" is "suffering [*pati*] with [*com*]." The term ordinarily refers to a mental state directed at another who is suffering, which involves a concern about their suffering, a concern for the good of the suffering individual. How might such a state have epistemological purchase? In what way does Murdoch understand *compassion* to have epistemological purchase?

As the question itself suggests, for Murdoch, viewing others with compassion has nothing to do with seeing only the good in them, or emphasizing their good qualities, or assuming that they possess good qualities. Although she thinks that

---

[83] Setiya questions "whether we can treat Murdoch's use of 'love' in the moral context as more than quixotic" (2013:19). Mason notes: "We tend to think that the very point of objective knowledge is to abstract away from any personal, particular point of view .... And we often think of love as a paradigm of just such a personal, particular – and perhaps distorted – point of view" (2021: 39). The resistance to Murdoch's position may reflect, in part, the continued influence of the liberal outlook in philosophy and in the wider culture (see Section 5).
[84] Murdoch uses the terms "love" and "compassion" interchangeably when describing the revelatory, or epistemological, power of love (S&G: 218; RZ: 142; OGG: 54–55; OGG: 65; SGC: 85).

individuals as such have value, we should not equate this with the idea that *every individual has good qualities*. When she says, for instance, that "if apprehension of good is apprehension of the individual and the real, then good partakes of the infinite elusive character of reality," Murdoch is not implying that individuals per se are good, but rather that it is always good to apprehend the reality of individuals (IP: 41). She affirms (among other things) the idea that "it's better to know what's real than to be in a state of fantasy or illusion" (OGG: 62).[85]

Compassion, for Murdoch, is realistic and judicious (e.g., IP: 37; OGG: 63–64; SGC: 85, 89). It involves "a clear-eyed contemplation of the misery and evil of the world" (OGG: 59). We can understand it as attuned, then, to the existential conditions that (on Murdoch's account) make reality difficult for human beings to face: our fragility, our lack of immunity to the depredations of time and chance, our inability to make perfect sense of things.[86] Seen this way, compassion has to do with viewing others in the light of these conditions, being *present to* these conditions in the lives of others and so, in a very real sense, to others as they are. It brings a depth of perspective, a steady recognition of the painful features of our condition as "human, historical individuals" (IP: 28; 3.4–3.5). It involves, Murdoch says, the sense that there is more to know about others: "[t]here is . . . something in the serious attempt to look compassionately at others which automatically suggests that 'there is more than this'" (SGC: 71).

One can regard another compassionately in *this* sense whether or not the other is visibly suffering, and whether or not she possesses (or one takes her to possess) any good qualities. In regarding someone compassionately one is both oriented to the good of the other, as "love" or "compassion" imply, and one gives due consideration to the individual's social and political context, as "justice" implies (Samuel 2021: esp. 321, n. 15). Such a form of love, finally, can be seen as working through imagination, through "reflection on people, events, etc., which builds detail, adds colour, conjures up possibilities," as when we imagine what someone's day, or childhood, might have been like (DPR: 198).

Many of these points come through in Murdoch's lovely review of *Dr. Zhivago*. She writes:

> The emergence of this book from Russia . . . is one of the best things which have happened for a long time. The story of the Revolution has often been told, more or less untruly . . .. One did not expect the privilege, and the

---

[85] Murdoch calls this position "realism." She also uses the term "realism" more descriptively (but still approvingly) to mean *the ability to perceive reality* (OGG: 64). She speaks of freedom from fantasy, for instance, as "the realism of compassion" (OGG: 65; also SGC: 85).

[86] "Goodness is connected with the acceptance of real death and real chance and real transience and only against the background of this acceptance, which is psychologically so difficult, can we understand the full extent of what virtue is like. The acceptance of death is . . . an automatic spur to our concern with what is not ourselves" (SGC: 100).

> education, of seeing it through the eyes of a great poet and, hereby, a great novelist . . . . Violence appears in the book, as it appears in life, absurd, ugly, highly contingent. Some deserters pursue an officer. He mounts a water butt to address them, and by this gesture checks them and gains their attention. He slips and half falls into the water butt. They burst out laughing and shoot him. This is how it is; and in his way of narrating these things the author conveys the real misery of life, where dramas never make complete sense and irrevocable losses come about by accident . . . . Zhivago [the character] is a tragic hero of a kind rarely achieved . . . . Though we vastly sympathize with him, we never excessively like, dislike, admire or despise him. He is an honest man, but not an especially heroic or purposeful one . . . . What he profoundly and movingly is is a human being, one who suffers the violence of events without being totally corrupted or totally destroyed (RZ: 140–141).

Murdoch here stresses the contingency of life, the fact of human suffering, the absence of a systematic pattern with which to "make complete sense" of this suffering, and our ability to "vastly sympathize" with others in this context.

She continues:

> A work such as [*Dr.*] *Zhivago* makes one realise how far a great artist can become the most profound consciousness of his time, deepening the understanding of his readers, and through this communion of understanding joining dissimilar peoples to each other. Seeking a name for the quality which makes this possible one is led to call it compassion, love. A writer can be remarkable without it; and where it is present in a great writer it is inseparable from his insight: whether he is looking at a marriage or a revolution or a cow tied up in a yard. This loving insight is present in [*Dr.*] *Zhivago* in great things and in small; in the sweep of the narrative which takes us through fifty such years . . . and in the tiny details which ravish the reader's delighted attention on every page (RZ: 142).

We see in this passage Murdoch's embrace of the idea that the knowing compassion that enables us to apprehend the reality of other people is identical to the knowing compassion that animates great art.[87] And we see how potent she takes such compassion to be: it has the potential to deepen understanding and thereby "[join] dissimilar peoples to each other."

4.4 Interlude

I've now considered love in relation to freedom and compassion. Let me step back and put things in broader perspective before considering love in relation to attention.

---

[87] This is one respect in which Murdoch considers morality and art ("goodness and beauty") to be "largely part of the same structure" (IP: 40). See Gomes 2013.

When Murdoch proposes that the individual is revealed by love, she is suggesting that we need love to get a true sense of what others are like and what it is like for them in situations of any complexity (Chappell 2018). This is not merely a matter of knowing facts (Mason 2023; Cordner 2016). We can know countless facts about a person or about the Nigerian Civil War without understanding, or even trying to understand, what it was like for that person to live through that event. The knowledge that love brings is not a clinical knowledge; it involves feeling and imagining our way into the experience of others in light of the bigger picture. Murdoch insists that the idea of love as revelatory is not a revolutionary or esoteric doctrine but a perfectly familiar idea, one that is borne out in the details of our daily lives and relationships: "In particular situations, 'reality' as that which is revealed to the patient eye of love is an idea entirely comprehensible to the ordinary person" (IP: 40; Forsberg 2024).

We're now in a position to appreciate one way that Murdoch considers her view to be importantly different from Kant's (while profoundly indebted to it). Kant, she believes, failed to properly recognize the emotions "as part of the structure of morality" (SGC: 79). So even though he associates practical reason with love – rightly, in Murdoch's view – he appeals to an emotionally sterile form of love (ibid.; S&G: 219–220). "He wants," Murdoch says, "to segregate the messy warm empirical psyche from the clean operations of ... reason" (SGC: 79).[88] Murdoch does not think such segregation is possible for human beings, or not always (nor does she think that we should necessarily aspire to it). For Murdoch, fully fledged reason engages desire, imagination, and compassion, especially when other persons are its object.

We're now also in a better position to see how, in keeping with the third postulate of the naturalistic outlook (which equates freedom with knowledge), the individual's knowledge of self and world could be *practical*. Since Murdoch connects the individual's knowledge to love, the conditions for arriving at this knowledge promise some degree of corresponding motivation. More plainly: for Murdoch, the work we must do to see other persons clearly – to circumvent fantasy – predisposes us to respond appropriately to what we see. Loving another, in Murdoch's sense, involves a *receptivity* to them, a felt presence to their unique being, and such receptivity predisposes one to be *motivated* by what one discovers. Thus: "[t]he more the separateness and differentness of other people is realized, and that fact seen that another man has needs and wishes as demanding as one's own, the harder it becomes to treat a person as a thing" (OGG: 64). For Murdoch, love reveals to us *the reality of others* and

---

[88] For an astute reading of Kant and Murdoch with respect to the moral importance of love, and for further references, see Merritt 2017.

this revelation is necessarily both freeing as well as constraining (and of course potentially motivating in other ways).[89]

4.5 Attention

Murdoch's concept of attention further illuminates what loving another amounts to. In the process, it crystallizes the interconnections between the uniqueness of individuals, their transcendence, and their need for love, both to know others and to be known by others. It thus serves as a capstone for Murdoch's naturalistic conception of the individual.

Murdoch's early writings note the importance of the concept of attention in Simone Weil's thought (KV; WG). In a notable moment in AD, Murdoch treats "attention" in a different way – as a desideratum for moral theory. She writes: "Simone Weil said that morality was a matter of attention, not will. We need a new vocabulary of attention" (AD: 293; Clarke 2013). It is not, however, until *Sovereignty* that the concept of attention figures in any substantive way in Murdoch's own philosophy. There we learn that the love that brings us knowledge of reality is typically exercised through *attention to individuals* and that such attention constitutes the main form of moral agency. "I have used the word 'attention,'" Murdoch says, "to express the idea of a just and loving gaze directed upon an individual reality. I believe this to be the characteristic and proper mark of the moral agent" (IP: 33). We learn further that the love in question involves a kind of self-suppression, that it is infinitely perfectible, and that it is singular. It will be helpful to examine each of these features in turn.

4.5.1 Self-Suppression

Some of the most striking moments in *Sovereignty* occur when Murdoch ties the achievement of knowledge and freedom to an overcoming or suppression of self. For instance:

> [S]uppression of self is required before accurate vision can be obtained (OGG: 65). Freedom, we find ... is the disciplined overcoming of self (SGC: 93).

Elsewhere, Murdoch says that the realism required for goodness "is automatically at the same time a suppression of self" (OGG: 64). And in SGC she speaks of "unselfing" to similar effect (82ff.).

Now it is to be expected that some kind of reining in of self will be required of creatures who are naturally egoistic. And it is hardly unusual to think of *love* as entailing such a curtailment of self. At the same time, when it comes to moral and

---

[89] Stern 2022 discusses the relation of freedom to choice in Murdoch's thought.

political matters, we may have reservations about the value of self-suppression and about remarks such as "we cease to be in order to attend to the existence of something else" (OGG: 58). David Bakhurst puts one worry this way:

> Unselfing is supposedly key to apprehending reality, including the reality of others. But how are we to understand interpersonal relations between selves seeking to countenance each other's reality? By abnegating myself, I am to recognize the reality of something that is itself trying to acknowledge my reality by negating itself – two fugitives in search of a meeting neither wishes to attend (2020: 219).

A related concern is that the last thing members of *subjugated* groups would seem to need, in many cases, is to be self-effacing or abnegating. They may need, rather, to have a stronger sense of self and of entitlement vis-à-vis members of dominant groups (Lovibond 2011; Hämäläinen 2015). The ideal of selflessness has played a particularly haunting role in the subjugation of women, for instance.

Fortunately, nothing forces us to identify unselfing with self-abnegation or with self-deprecation.[90] Rather, when we unself we focus on something outside the self and consider it noninstrumentally. We regard it apart from what it can do for us or what it means to us. We *contemplate* it (OGG: 63–64). Murdoch's point is that, for creatures like us – creatures who must contend with the relentless machinations of the psyche as we negotiate a fraught and complicated world – to regard another (or a situation) in this disinterested way just is a kind of self-suppression. We can think of unselfing as the other side of absorption. To be absorbed in another involves, or may involve, a temporary relinquishment of the space that the self normally occupies. Equally, we can think of unselfing as emotional and imaginative engagement with another being that is not directed by self-interest, that is not possessive.[91] It is certainly compatible with (and likely a precondition for) a healthy self-regard.

Murdoch, however, does not think that we can simply *will* ourselves into a loving and disinterested point of view (or state of being); the will, in her view, is too beholden to the psyche (3.5; OGG: 65; SGC: 89). Her thought is that we can *direct our gaze* in such a way as to make our achievement of such a state more likely.[92] The important thing, as she sees it, is for one's gaze to be trained

---

[90] For an overview of the texts and analysis, see Panizza 2022: chaps. 2 and 3; Antonaccio 2000: 135–142.

[91] Regarding others noninstrumentally means not only that we value them apart from *our own* ends (hence "unselfing"), but also that we value them apart from any contribution they make to a socio-cosmological order, as Keaja and Tselane came to value each other. I am grateful to an anonymous referee for this point.

[92] "Man is not a combination of an impersonal rational thinker and a personal will. He is a unified being who sees, and who has some continual slight control over the direction and focus of his vision" (IP: 39).

on something specific that is not oneself (OGG: 58). So trained, our gaze may reward us with an apprehension of our object that isn't skewed by the unchecked presence of self and by any accompanying energy.

Seemingly anything outside the self can be an occasion for unselfing or self-suppression: a work of art, an animal seen from a distance, a foreign language, even a stone or blade of grass (SGC: 83, 86).[93] Put another way, Murdoch believes that reality avoidance can distort our perception of anything. She believes it is most likely, however, to distort our perception of other persons. It is fitting, then, that Murdoch's chief illustration of attention involves two persons: a mother-in-law (M) and a daughter-in-law (D). In what has become a very famous example, M overcomes a snobby and crabbed view of D (as coarse, immature) in favor of a more judicious appraisal (as unpretentious, playful) (IP: 16–19). M does this not by gathering new information about D in a clinical way, or by being rationally persuaded of D's merits through argument, but by training a just and loving "gaze" on her, by putting her anxieties or expectations to the side and reconsidering D with greater care and perspective.[94] This particular kind of action, Murdoch submits, brings her real knowledge of D. "When M is just and loving, she sees D as she really is" (IP: 37; cf. Hopwood 2017).

The example of M and D also serves to emphasize two other aspects of love that Murdoch considers essential: its infinite perfectibility and its singularity.[95]

4.5.2 Infinite Perfectibility

To say that love is infinitely perfectible is to say that the endeavor to reach a fully adequate understanding of another individual is never-ending. "M confronted with D has an endless task" (IP: 39). Murdoch takes the infinite perfectibility of love to be both a feature of ordinary experience and a familiar ideal.[96] We simply do find, Murdoch maintains, that truly understanding another person – forming a just conception of another person – requires effort and compassion, and that this

---

[93] This, I suggest, is what defines "individual realities" in Murdoch's lexicon. An individual reality is anything whose apprehension requires or rewards unselfing. Murdoch believes this to be most obviously true of other persons. Notably, one's *own* self is not an individual reality for Murdoch; self is not, for her, a proper object of attention. For critical discussion of this point, see Milligan 2022; Pendleton 2022; Mole 2007; Vice 2007.
[94] Pendleton 2022 points out that Murdoch intends "gaze" as a metaphor – not literally – and discusses some of the metaphor's limitations.
[95] Strictly, the example is meant to disprove the thesis (what Murdoch calls the "genetic theory of meaning") that we grasp the meaning of moral concepts *fully* when we learn their ordinary *public* meaning.
[96] "Since we are neither angels nor animals but human individuals, our dealings with each other have this aspect; and this may be regarded as an empirical fact or ... as a synthetic *a priori* truth" (IP: 27). See 3.1.

work is progressive and never complete. "M knows what she is doing when she tries to be just to D, and we know what she is doing, too," Murdoch says (IP: 39). The uniqueness of individuals, their historical nature, their egocentricity, and the elusiveness of reality all help elucidate *why* the activity of forming an adequate understanding of others is never finished, on Murdoch's account, and why it is a task. Love is the endeavor by one human, historical – and egocentric – individual to be just to another such individual, in the midst of a scene that neither individual can ever nail down. Love is "the pursuit of the individual by the individual" in a huge and chancy world (IP: 41; Mylonakai 2019). Such a pursuit is bound to be ongoing and demanding.

Murdoch further emphasizes the progressive nature of love in *Sovereignty* by drawing systematic links between (a) the concept of love, (b) the concepts of the individual or reality, and (c) the concept of perfection or good.[97] *Love*, she maintains, consists in the endeavor by the *individual* to reach a *better* – ever more *perfect* – knowledge of *reality*, where the prime embodiment of reality is other human *individuals*. Thus: "The central concept of morality is 'the individual' thought of as knowable by love in the light of the command 'Be ye therefore perfect'" (IP: 29).[98] Or, substituting the concept of *good* for that of *perfection*, we could put it this way: love consists in the endeavor on the part of the individual to see other individuals in the light of the *good* – where good is uncodifiable and magnetic – and the central concept of morality is precisely that of the individual as knowable in this particular way (IP: 41; OGG: 68–70). To keep a firm grasp on Murdoch's point, it is important not to conflate "more perfect knowledge" of others with just *any* increase in our knowledge about them. This, we might say, was Mr. Capaldi's mistake. He couldn't see that *merely knowing about* Josie was not the same as *knowing* Josie, and so he also couldn't see that those who love her might know her (and know about her) better than he – who approached her as a science project-cum-commodity – ever could.

It may well be the infinite perfectibility of love, more than anything, that led Murdoch to have second thoughts about whether moral philosophy should, in fact, be used to generate political views.[99] Murdoch was particularly wary of the idea that the state should seek to *perfect* itself or its members, an idea she

---

[97] "As soon as we begin to use words such as 'love' and 'justice' in characterizing M," says Murdoch, "we introduce into our whole conceptual picture of her situation the idea of progress, that is the idea of perfection" (IP: 23). "I want here to connect two ideas, the idea of the individual and the idea of perfection" (IP: 27). "Good. Real. Love. These words are closely connected" (IP: 41).

[98] Murdoch is referring to Matthew 5:48: "Be ye therefore perfect, even as your Father which is in heaven is perfect" (King James Version). For context for this passage, see Merritt 2017: n. 33.

[99] *Sovereignty*'s introduction of the concept of the psyche might also have contributed to Murdoch's reservations in this connection (given her concern to protect the individual from coercion). Others have raised concerns about the political implications of Murdoch's theory of

associated with the disastrous utopianism of the former Soviet Union and the People's Republic of China (Browning 2019). Although Murdoch did not emphasize this point until MGM, it surfaces, we may recall from 1.5, in her comments in the postscript to OGG:

> The idea of excellence has ... a different operation in morals from its operation in politics, since a final acceptance of imperfection and incompleteness is built into politics in a way in which it is not built into personal morals. The command "Be perfect," which can never do harm to the artist or the moral agent, is a very dangerous political slogan (PSP: 6).

So we need to bear in mind that however much the practice of just and loving attention might contribute to a democratic way of life, Murdoch does not intend for just and loving attention to be (somehow) instrumentalized by the state.[100] Individuals should try to perfect their understandings, in her view, but states or communities should not try to perfect their members. No one should be forced to be free. Nor should the state seek to perfect *itself* at the expense of individual members. This brings us, finally, to the singularity of love.

4.5.3 Singularity

To say that love is singular, on Murdoch's account, is to say that the activity of loving another is uncodifiable, individual-specific, not conformable to a timeless or universal pattern. Efforts of loving attention proceed from a continuous, evolving "fabric of being" that is unique and once only (IP: 29). "M's activity is peculiarly *her own*. Its details are the details of *this* personality" (IP: 22).[101] More precisely, we could say, the details of M's attention to D are the details of *this* personality dealing with *that* object at *this* particular time. Of course, exercises of loving attention must meet certain conditions. They must be disinterested and compassionate, but they can take countless forms and are nonrepeatable because they are exercised by and toward "human, historical individuals." This, Murdoch notes, "makes it difficult to learn goodness from another person" (IP: 29).

The singularity of love also marks what Murdoch sees as a second major difference between her picture of morality and Kant's. She famously observes: "Kant does not tell us to respect whole particular tangled-up historical

---

the good, which was also first articulated in *Sovereignty*. See Antonaccio 2012: ch. 8 for discussion of these concerns and references.

[100] Laverty 2022 and Spreeuwenberg 2021 defend the civic value of loving attention in ways that are sensitive to this constraint.

[101] "M's activity is hard to characterize not because it is hazy but *precisely because it is moral*" (IP: 22). M's activity is hard to characterize, that is, because it is an exercise of *love* and thus individual- and context-specific. (And partly for that reason, Murdoch notes, it may also be "private" or unobservable.)

individuals, but to respect the universal reason in their breasts." She adds that, for Kant, "[i]n so far as we are rational and moral we are all the same, and in some mysterious sense transcendent to history" (S&G: 215). For Murdoch, as we have seen, we are mysterious to one another in part precisely *because* we are very much *not* transcendent to history. We are creatures of a specific time, place, and context. As a result, Murdoch thinks, there is no timeless one-size-fits-all pattern for exercises of love and respect to follow; such exercises must be various and singular, like the individuals they help to connect.

Summarizing. The concept of attention crystallizes Murdoch's development of the idea that "love ... is the discovery of reality." It *also* joins together the different features of Murdoch's conception of the individual – his uniqueness, his unsurveyability, and his dependence on love if he is to see others justly or be seen justly by others. We learn from Murdoch's discussion that the love that discloses reality will be expressed differently by different individuals in different contexts, but that it will characteristically take the form of attention, that it will involve a contemplative stance, an awareness of human fragility, and the sense that there is more to know. We learn that attention's prime object will be other "human, historical individuals," who themselves need to engage in the same discipline if they are not to be prisoners of their own, or their society's, worst evasions of reality.

4.6 Love and Politics

Having considered in this section the importance that Murdoch assigns to love for reaching an adequate perception of the individual, I want to return to issues I raised at the end of Section 3. We are now in a better position to see why Murdoch thinks that love belongs with her concept of the individual and why love is not necessarily out of place where politics is concerned.

On reflection, it makes a good deal of sense to view the idea that individuals are knowable through love, the idea that they are unique, and the idea that they are transcendent as *jointly* involved in a liberal sensibility. Seeing others as unique and transcendent does not guarantee an appreciation of their "right to exist and to have a separate mode of being which is important and interesting to themselves" (SBR: 257/271). For *that*, Murdoch suggests, one also needs to appreciate their fragility, a fragility one shares in. And this, she thinks, requires love. "We are all mortal," Murdoch says, "and equally at the mercy of necessity and chance. These are the true aspects in which all men are brothers" (OGG: 72). Here we may remember that the motto of the French Revolution was not "liberté, égalité" but rather "liberté, égalité, fraternité." The loving insight that Murdoch associates with the liberal spirit has a strong claim to be a form of brotherly – or sisterly – love.

5 Concluding Remarks

[W]hat we require is a renewed sense of the difficulty and complexity of the moral life and the opacity of persons.[102]

Readers have long underestimated the political significance of Murdoch's moral thought. This is partly because Murdoch's earlier writings, in which there is far more engagement with political issues, have been overshadowed by the essays in *Sovereignty* and because these later essays speak so powerfully to the desire to make oneself a better person through one's individual efforts. But to neglect the political dimensions of Murdoch's ethics is to underestimate the reach, the complexity, and the coherence of her philosophical vision. It is to miss how seamlessly Murdoch's focus on the inner life fits with her commitment to Enlightenment ideals.

Murdoch's early writings focus on an *internal* threat to these ideals, the threat of the *modern* or "liberal" outlook that was inspired by the Enlightenment and nourished by the remarkable successes of modern science and the concomitant diminution of religious authority. In a kind of paradox, Murdoch sees the liberal outlook as itself posing a threat to the ideas and practices that sustain a liberal sensibility. Her concept of the individual is designed, in part, to counter this threat. It enjoins us to see other individuals as more than any description we might form of them, as subject to the same painful predicaments and vicissitudes as we ourselves are, and, ultimately, as beings who are importantly different from one another. The point is not to *like* others but to avoid (or to get past) conceptions of them that may blind us to the real possibilities for peaceful coexistence.

In assessing the contemporary significance of Murdoch's project, we should note that not all four postulates of the liberal outlook continue to enjoy prominence today. In particular, behaviorism (expressed in postulate 4L) is not the intellectual or cultural force it was in Murdoch's day and there is, correspondingly, a greater willingness to recognize the reality and importance of the inner life. Murdoch herself may be partly to thank for this. But the separation of fact from value, the identification of freedom with doing what one wants, and the idea of the individual as endowing the world with value – in effect, postulates 1L, 2L, and 3L – are alive and well. The problem, as Murdoch sees it, is that the picture formed by these ideas leaves no room for the idea that *others*

---

[102] AD: 293.

transcend us in a meaningful way. Without this idea, Murdoch thinks, we will not be inclined to treat our perceptions of others with due circumspection, or to feel due curiosity about their lives and their motives. We will not be primed to experience their reality.

We should also note that Murdoch's concept of the individual depends on ideas that are disputable, such as the idea that reality is elusive or the idea that love is progressive and revelatory. Murdoch's picture will, I think, be very helpful to members of the liberal world who embrace these ideas. For those who reject them – whether because they are deeply committed to the liberal outlook or for other reasons – but still wish to affirm Enlightenment political ideals, Murdoch sets a challenge and offers potential assistance. She challenges them to articulate a picture of individuals that would better serve a liberal democratic way of life, or to show why this is not necessary, and she offers them an incredibly rich starting point from which to do that. In this way, I think, Murdoch succeeds in doing precisely what she thinks philosophy should do: help us to reach the concepts we need to live our best lives, separately and together, in the world as it is.

Abbreviations of Works by Murdoch

For the three essays that comprise *The Sovereignty of Good* (IP, OGG, and SGC), page numbers are given for the 1970 book publication (SG). For the essays VC and SBR, page numbers are given for the original essays and then, following a forward slash, for the reprinted versions in EM. (The reprints of these two essays omit some of the original text, so in some cases only the original page numbers appear.) Page numbers for all other texts that appear in EM correspond to the versions reprinted there.

AD	"Against Dryness" (1961). In EM: 287–295.
DPR	"The Darkness of Practical Reason" (1966). In EM: 193–202.
EH	"The Existentialist Hero" (1950). In EM: 108–115.
EM	*Existentialists and Mystics: Writings on Philosophy and Literature* (1997), ed. P. Conradi. New York: Penguin Books.
EPM	"The Existentialist Political Myth" (1952). In EM: 130–145.
HMD	"Hegel in Modern Dress" (1957). In EM: 146–150.
HT	"A House of Theory" (1958). In EM: 171–186.
IP	"The Idea of Perfection" (1964). In SG: 1–44.
KV	"'Knowing the Void': Review of Simone Weil's Notebooks" (1956). In EM: 157–160.
MB	"Morality and the Bomb" (1962). In *Occasional Essays by Iris Murdoch* (1998), ed. Y. Muroya and P. Hullah. Okoyama: University Education Press, pp. 21–27.
MDH	"The Moral Decision about Homosexuality" (1964). In *Occasional Essays by Iris Murdoch* (1998), ed. Y. Muroya and P. Hullah. Okoyama: University Education Press, pp. 31–38.
ME	"Metaphysics and Ethics" (1957). In EM: 59–75.
MGM	*Metaphysics as a Guide to Morals* (1992). New York: Penguin.
NM	"The Novelist as Metaphysician" (1950). In EM: 101–107.
NP	"Nostalgia for the Particular" (1951–1952). In EM: 43–58.
OGG	"On 'God' and 'Good'" (1969). In SG: 45–74.
PM	"Political Morality and the War in Vietnam" (1967). *Quadrant* 11(3): 7–9.
PSP	"Postscript [to 'On "God" and "Good"'] on Politics" (1966). With Introductory Note by J. Broackes. *Iris Murdoch Review* 1(3) (2011): 6–8.
RZ	"Review of *Dr. Zhivago*" (1958). *The New Reasoner* 7: 140–142.

SBR	"The Sublime and the Beautiful Revisited" (1959). *Yale Review* 49(2): 247–271. In EM: 261–286.
SG	*The Sovereignty of Good* (1970). London: Routledge.
S&G	"The Sublime and the Good" (1959). In EM: 205–220.
SGC	"The Sovereignty of Good over Other Concepts" (1967). In SG: 75–101.
SSR	*Sartre: Romantic Rationalist* (1987) [1953]. Reprint. New York: Viking Penguin.
TL	"Thinking and Language" (1951). In EM: 33–42.
TSM	"T. S. Eliot as a Moralist" (1958). In EM: 161–170.
VC	"Vision and Choice in Morality" (1956). *Proceedings of the Aristotelian* Society (suppl.), 30: 32–58. In EM: 76–98.
WG	"Waiting on God: A Radio Talk on Simone Weil" (1951). *Iris Murdoch Review* 8 (2017): 9–16.

References

Antonaccio, M. (2000). *Picturing the Human*. Oxford: Oxford University Press.
Antonaccio, M. (2002). The Moral and Political Imagination of Iris Murdoch. *Notizie di Politeia* 18(66): 22–50.
Antonaccio, M. (2012). *A Philosophy to Live By*. Oxford: Oxford University Press.
Antonaccio, M. and Schweiker, W. (eds.) (1996). *Iris Murdoch and the Search for Human Goodness*. Chicago: University of Chicago Press.
Appiah, K. A. (1990). Racisms. In D. Goldberg, ed., *Anatomy of Racism*. Minneapolis: University of Minnesota Press, pp. 3–17.
Aziz, R. (2010). *The Two Faces of American Freedom*. Cambridge, MA: Harvard University Press.
Bakhurst, D. (2020). Analysis and Transcendence in *The Sovereignty of Good*. *European Journal of Philosophy* 28(1): 214–223.
Bilgrami, A. (2014). *Secularism, Identity, and Enchantment*. Cambridge, MA: Harvard University Press.
Blum, L. (2022a). Iris Murdoch. In E. N. Zalta, ed., *Stanford Encyclopedia of Philosophy*, Winter 2022 edition. https://plato.stanford.edu/archives/win2022/entries/murdoch/.
Blum, L. (2022b). Murdoch and Politics. In M. Hopwood and S. Panizza, eds., *The Murdochian Mind*. New York: Routledge, pp. 424–437.
Bolton, L. (2022). Murdoch and Feminism. In M. Hopwood and S. Panizza, eds., *The Murdochian Mind*. New York: Routledge, pp. 438–450.
Broackes, J. (2012). Introduction. In J. Broackes, ed., *Iris Murdoch, Philosopher*. Oxford: Oxford University Press, pp. 1–92.
Browning, G. (2018a). *Why Iris Murdoch Matters*. London: Bloomsbury.
Browning, G. (2018b). Murdoch and the End of Ideology. In G. Browning, ed., *Murdoch on Truth and Love*. Basingstoke: Palgrave Macmillan, pp. 133–157.
Browning, G. (2019). The Metaphysics of Morals and Politics. In N. Hämäläinen and G. Dooley, eds., *Reading Iris Murdoch's Metaphysics as a Guide to Morals*. Basingstoke: Palgrave Macmillan, pp. 179–194.
Browning, G. (2024). *Iris Murdoch and the Political*. Oxford: Oxford University Press.
Chappell, S. (2018). Love and Knowledge in Murdoch. In G. Browning, ed., *Murdoch on Truth and Love*. Basingstoke: Palgrave Macmillan, pp. 89–108.

Clarke, B. (2006). Iris Murdoch and the Politics of Imagination. *Philosophical Papers* 35(3): 387–411.

Clarke, B. (2012). Iris Murdoch and the Prospects for Critical Moral Perception. In J. Broackes, ed., *Iris Murdoch, Philosopher*. Oxford: Oxford University Press, pp. 227–253.

Clarke, B. (2013). Attention, Moral. In H. LaFollette, ed., *International Encyclopedia of Ethics*. Oxford: Wiley Blackwell, pp. 388–392. https://doi.org/10.1002/9781444367072.wbiee403.

Clarke, B. (2018). Iris Murdoch and the Meaning of Life. In S. Leach and J. Tartaglia, eds., *The Meaning of Life and the Great Philosophers*. New York: Routledge, pp. 252–259.

Coates, T. (2015). What This Cruel War Was Over. *The Atlantic Monthly*. www.theatlantic.com/politics/archive/2015/06/what-this-cruel-war-was-over/396482/.

Conradi, P. (2001). *Iris: The Life of Iris Murdoch*. New York: W.W. Norton.

Cordner, C. (2016). Lessons of Murdochian Attention. *Sophia* 55(2): 197–213.

Cordner, C. (2022). Love. In M. Hopwood and S. Panizza, eds., *The Murdochian Mind*. New York: Routledge, pp. 169–182.

Dewey, J. (1988) [1939]. Creative Democracy: The Task Before Us. In J. Boydston, ed., *The Later Works, 1925–1953*, vol. 14. Carbondale: Southern Illinois University Press, pp. 224–230.

Diamond, C. (1988). Losing Your Concepts. *Ethics* 98(2): 255–277.

Diamond, C. (1996). "We Are Perpetually Moralists": Iris Murdoch, Fact, and Value. In M. Antonaccio and W. Schweiker, eds., *Iris Murdoch and the Search for Human Goodness*. Chicago: University of Chicago Press, pp. 79–109.

Diamond, C. (2010). Murdoch the Explorer. *Philosophical Topics* 38(1): 51–85.

Dumont, L. (1980). *Homo Hierarchus: The Caste System and Its Implications*, trans. M. Sainsbury, L. Dumont, and B. Gulati. Revised English edition. Chicago: University of Chicago Press.

Dumont, L. (1986). *Essays on Individualism*. Chicago: University of Chicago Press.

Elkins, C. (2022). *A Legacy of Violence*. New York: Alfred A. Knopf.

Forsberg, N. (2013). *Language Lost and Found: On Iris Murdoch and the Limits of Philosophical Discourse*. London: Bloomsbury.

Forsberg, N. (2024). Iris Murdoch on Love. In C. Grau and A. Smuts, eds., *The Oxford Handbook of the Philosophy of Love*. Oxford: Oxford University Press, pp. 432–450.

Fredrickson, G. (2002). *Racism: A Short History*. Princeton: Princeton University Press.

Gomes, A. (2013). Iris Murdoch on Art, Ethics, and Attention. *British Journal of Aesthetics* 53(3): 321–337.

Gomes, A. (2025, forthcoming). Iris Murdoch on Privacy, Perfection, and the Philosophy of Mind. In C. Bagnoli and B. Cokelet, eds., *Murdoch's The Sovereignty of Good at 55*. Cambridge: Cambridge University Press.

Hahn, S. (2024). *Illiberal America*. New York: W.W. Norton.

Hämäläinen, N. (2015). Reduce Ourselves to Zero? Sabina Lovibond, Iris Murdoch, and Feminism. *Hypatia* 30(4): 743–759.

Hämäläinen, N. (2022). Murdoch on Ethical Formation in a Changing World. *Journal of Philosophy of Education* 56: 827–837.

Head, B. (1990). The Lovers. In *Tales of Tenderness and Power*. Oxford: Heinemann, pp. 84–101.

Holland, M. (2012). Social Convention and Neurosis as Obstacles to Moral Freedom. In J. Broackes, ed., *Iris Murdoch, Philosopher*. Oxford: Oxford University Press, pp. 255–274.

Hopwood, M. (2017). "The Extremely Difficult Realization that Something Other than Oneself Is Real": Iris Murdoch on Love and Moral Agency. *European Journal of Philosophy* 26(1): 477–501.

Horner, A. and Rowe, A. (eds.) (2016). *Living on Paper: Letters from Iris Murdoch, 1934–1995*. Princeton: Princeton University Press.

Ishiguro, K. (2021). *Klara and the Sun*. New York: Alfred A. Knopf.

Jamieson, L. (2023). *Iris Murdoch's Practical Metaphysics*. London: Palgrave Macmillan.

John, E. (2013). Love and the Need for Comprehension. *Philosophical Explorations* 16(3): 285–297.

Jones, R. P. (2021). *White Too Long: The Legacy of White Supremacy in American Christianity*. New York: Simon & Schuster.

Kincaid, J. (1990). *Lucy*. New York: Farrar, Straus and Giroux.

Kreuz, R. (2023). How the Unabomber's Unique Linguistic Fingerprints Led to His Capture. *The Conversation*. https://theconversation.com/how-the-unabombers-unique-linguistic-fingerprints-led-to-his-capture-207681.

Langton, R. (1992). Duty and Desolation. *Philosophy* 67(262): 481–505.

Laverty, M. (2022). Civility. In M. Hopwood and S. Panizza, eds., *The Murdochian Mind*. New York: Routledge, pp. 505–518.

Lipscomb, J. B. (2022). *The Women Are Up to Something*. Oxford: Oxford University Press.

Lopez, B. (2001). *Arctic Dreams*. Reprint. New York: Vintage.

Lovibond, S. (2011). *Iris Murdoch, Gender and Philosophy*. New York: Routledge.

MacCumhaill, C. M. and Wiseman, R. (2022). *Metaphysical Animals*. New York: Doubleday.

Manguso, S. (2017). *300 Arguments*. Minneapolis: Graywolf Press.

Mason, C. (2021). Iris Murdoch and the Epistemic Significance of Love. In S. Cushing, ed., *New Philosophical Essays on Love and Loving*. Cham: Palgrave Macmillan, pp. 39–62.

Mason, C. (2023). Reconceiving Murdochian Realism. *Ergo: An Open Access Journal of Philosophy* 10(23): 649–672.

McCann, C. (2020). *Apeirogon*. New York: Random House.

McCurry, S. (2020). The Confederacy Was an Antidemocratic, Centralized State. *The Atlantic Monthly*. www.theatlantic.com/ideas/archive/2020/06/confederacy-wasnt-what-you-think/613309/.

Merritt, M. (2017). Love, Respect, and Individuals: Murdoch as a Guide to Kantian Ethics. *European Journal of Philosophy* 25(4): 1844–1863.

Merritt, M. (2022). Murdoch and Kant. In M. Hopwood and S. Panizza, eds., *The Murdochian Mind*. New York: Routledge, pp. 253–265.

Mill, J. S. (1978) [1859]. *On Liberty*. Indianapolis: Hackett.

Milligan, T. (2022). Loving Attention to Animals. In M. Hopwood and S. Panizza, eds., *The Murdochian Mind*. New York: Routledge, pp. 468–478.

Mole, C. (2007). Attention, Self and *The Sovereignty of Good*. In A. Rowe, ed., *Iris Murdoch: A Reassessment*. London: Palgrave Macmillan, pp. 72–84.

Mylonaki, E. (2019). "The Individual in Pursuit of the Individual": A Murdochian Account of Moral Perception. *The Journal of Value Inquiry* 53(4): 579–603.

Nussbaum, M. (2001). "When She Was Good." *The New Republic*. https://newrepublic.com/article/122264/iris-murdoch-novelist-and-philospher.

Panizza, S. (2020). Moral Perception beyond Supervenience: Iris Murdoch's Radical Perspective. *The Journal of Value Inquiry* 54(2): 273–288.

Panizza, S. (2022). *The Ethics of Attention*. New York: Routledge.

Pendleton, H. (2022). How to See: The Gaze in Iris Murdoch's Moral Philosophy. In S. Wuppuluri and A. C. Grayling, eds., *Metaphors and Analogies in Sciences and Humanities: Words and Worlds*. Cham: Springer Publishing AG, pp. 499–522.

Rich, A. (1979). Women and Honor: Some Notes on Lying. In *Lies, Secrets and Silence*. New York: W.W. Norton, pp. 185–194.

Robjant, D. (2011). Is Iris Murdoch an Unconscious Misogynist? *The Heythrop Journal* 52: 1021–1031.

Samuel, J. (2021). Thin as a Needle, Quick as a Flash: Murdoch on Agency and Moral Progress. *The Review of Metaphysics* 75(2): 345–373.

Sanchez-Schilling, S. (2019). The Politics of an Aestheticized Ethics. Unpublished. Presented at the Iris Murdoch Centenary Conference. St. Anne's College, Oxford.

Setiya, K. (2013). Murdoch on the Sovereignty of Good. *Philosophers' Imprint* 3: 1–21.

Setiya, K. (2024). Is Philosophy Self-Help? *The Point*. https://thepointmag.com/examined-life/is-philosophy-self-help/?utm_source=substack&utm_medium=email.

Spreeuwenberg, L. (2021). "Love" as a Practice: Looking at Real People. In S. Cushing, ed., *New Philosophical Essays on Love and Loving*. Cham: Palgrave MacMillan, pp. 63–86.

Stern, R. (2022). "How Is Human Freedom Compatible with the Authority of the Good?" Murdoch on Moral Agency, Freedom, and Imagination. *Proceedings of the Aristotelian Society* 122(1): 1–26.

Streep, A. (2023). How Montana Took a Hard Right toward Christian Nationalism. *New York Times Sunday Magazine*. www.nytimes.com/2023/01/11/magazine/montana-republicans-christian-nationalism.html?unlocked_article_code=1.9E0.CO1K.3c3qfaGFWM6D&smid=url-share.

Vecchione, J. (dir.) (1987). *Fighting Back (1957–1962). Eyes on the Prize*. Blackside, Inc. PBS Video.

Vice, S. (2007). The Ethics of Self-Concern. In A. Rowe, ed., *Iris Murdoch: A Reassessment*. London: Palgrave Macmillan, pp. 60–71.

Walzer, M. (2023). *The Struggle for a Decent Politics: On "Liberal" as an Adjective*. New Haven: Yale University Press.

Weil, S. (1978) [1951]. *Waiting for God*, trans. E. Craufurd. New York: Harper Collins.

Weil, S. (2002) [1952]. *Gravity and Grace*, trans. E. Crawford and M. von der Ruhr. New York: Routledge.

Wilkerson, I. (2020). *Caste: The Origins of Our Discontent*. New York: Random House.

Wiseman, R. (2020). What If the Private Linguist Were a Poet? Iris Murdoch on Privacy and Ethics. *European Journal of Philosophy* 28(1): 224–234.

Woodhead, L. (dir.) (2019). *Just One of Those Things*. Eagle Rock Films.

Zakaria, F. (1997). The Rise of Illiberal Democracy. *Foreign Affairs* 76(6): 22–43.

Acknowledgments

I wrote the first draft of this Element while on sabbatical with my family at the University of Iceland in 2022–2023. Many thanks to the University of Montana for the sabbatical award and to the Department of Philosophy in Reykjavík for providing a lovely environment in which to spend it. Róbert Haraldsson and Kolbrún Pállsdóttir inspired our visit and saw to our every need in their beautiful country; I am deeply grateful for their friendship, and for that of Amélie Rorty (1932–2020), who is missed. My recent thinking about Murdoch has been particularly enriched by the students in my Murdoch seminars at the University of Montana and by a series of talks on moral attention that took place at the University of Fribourg in 2018 and 2021. I am indebted to Maude Oullette-Dubé for organizing these talks and for inviting me to join them. Maude also provided valuable comments on a draft of this Element, as did Jacqueline Broad, Anil Gomes, and two anonymous readers for Cambridge. Paul Muench read early as well as later versions of these pages and improved them immeasurably. Ella gave me vital perspective. My loving gratitude to all the family and friends who sustain me.

For P.

Cambridge Elements ≡

Women in the History of Philosophy

Jacqueline Broad
Monash University

Jacqueline Broad is Professor of Philosophy at Monash University, Australia. Her area of expertise is early modern philosophy, with a special focus on seventeenth and eighteenth-century women philosophers. She is the author of *Women Philosophers of the Seventeenth Century* (Cambridge University Press, 2002), *A History of Women's Political Thought in Europe, 1400–1700* (with Karen Green; Cambridge University Press, 2009), and *The Philosophy of Mary Astell: An Early Modern Theory of Virtue* (Oxford University Press, 2015).

Advisory Board

Dirk Baltzly, *University of Tasmania*
Sandrine Bergès, *Bilkent University*
Marguerite Deslauriers, *McGill University*
Karen Green, *University of Melbourne*
Lisa Shapiro, *McGill University*
Emily Thomas, *Durham University*

About the Series

In this Cambridge Elements series, distinguished authors provide concise and structured introductions to a comprehensive range of prominent and lesser-known figures in the history of women's philosophical endeavour, from ancient times to the present day.

Cambridge Elements

Women in the History of Philosophy

Elements in the Series

Im Yunjidang
Sungmoon Kim

Early Christian Women
Dawn LaValle Norman

Mary Shepherd
Antonia LoLordo

Mary Wollstonecraft
Martina Reuter

Susan Stebbing
Frederique Janssen-Lauret

Harriet Taylor Mill
Helen McCabe

Victoria Welby
Emily Thomas

Nísia Floresta
Nastassja Pugliese

Catharine Trotter Cockburn
Ruth Boeker

Lucrezia Marinella
Marguerite Deslauriers

Amalia Holst
Andrew Cooper

Iris Murdoch
Bridget Clarke

A full series listing is available at: www.cambridge.org/EWHP

For EU product safety concerns, contact us at Calle de José Abascal, 56–1°, 28003 Madrid, Spain or eugpsr@cambridge.org.

www.ingramcontent.com/pod-product-compliance
Ingram Content Group UK Ltd.
Pitfield, Milton Keynes, MK11 3LW, UK
UKHW020056310525
458926UK00016B/212